THE COMPLETE
GOOD ENERGY
COOKBOOK

101 Metabolism-Boosting Recipes to Optimize Your Health for Longevity and Feel Incredible at Every Age

Dr. Rachel C. Jenkins

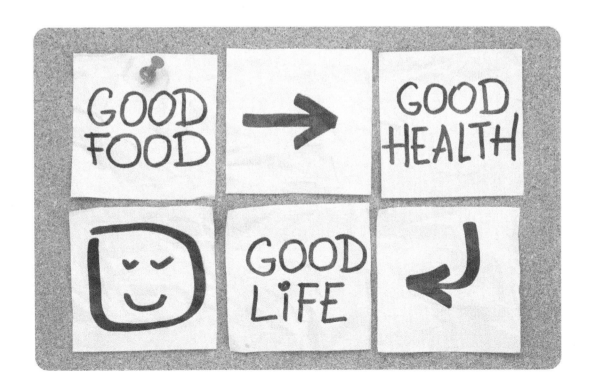

Contents

Dedication 4

Acknowledgement 4

Introduction 5

How to Use This Cookbook 6

How This Cookbook Can Help You 6

The Good Energy Philosophy 7

The Importance of Metabolic Health in Everyday Cooking 7

Understanding Good Energy 8

Key Principles of Good Energy Eating 8

Tips for Stocking a Good Energy Kitchen 9

Lifestyle Tips for Good Energy 10

BREAKFAST RECIPES 11

LUNCH RECIPES 27

DINNER RECIPES 43

SNACKS AND APPETIZERS 57

DESSERTS RECIPES 71

DRINKS RECIPES 85

How to Plan a Week of Good Energy Meals 97

Tips for Efficient Meal Prep 98

GOOD ENERGY FOOD LISTS 99

30-DAY MEAL PLAN 101

Recipes Index 105

Conclusion 108

Bonus 108

Dedication

This book is dedicated to all those seeking a healthier, more vibrant life. To those who believe in the power of food as medicine, and to everyone striving to create "good energy" in their bodies and minds—this book is for you. May it bring joy, health, and delicious meals to your table.

Acknowledgement

This book has been a journey of passion, curiosity, and a deep commitment to better health. First and foremost, I want to thank Dr. Casey Means for her groundbreaking work and for inspiring a new approach to wellness that aligns with the principles of Good Energy. Your insights and research have laid the foundation for this cookbook, and I'm grateful for the clarity and wisdom you bring to the conversation about metabolic health.

To my family and friends, thank you for your unwavering support and for being my biggest taste-testers. Your feedback, patience, and encouragement have been invaluable throughout this process.

A special thank you to the dedicated team behind this book—editors, designers, and everyone who played a part in bringing this project to life. Your expertise and hard work have made this book what it is today.

And to you, the reader—thank you for choosing to embark on this journey toward better health with me. Your commitment to nourishing yourself and your loved ones with Good Energy is both inspiring and motivating. I hope this book serves as a trusted guide in your kitchen and in your life.

Introduction

Welcome to a journey that's going to change the way you think about food, energy, and health. I'm thrilled to guide you through the world of Good Energy Cooking, where every dish is crafted with your body's best interests at heart. As someone who has spent years in the kitchen, both professionally and at home, I can tell you that cooking isn't just about feeding the body—it's about nourishing the soul.

In this cookbook, we're going to dive into recipes that don't just taste great but also align with the principles of Good Energy as taught by Dr. Casey Means in her groundbreaking work, Good Energy: The Surprising Connection Between Metabolism and Limitless Health. These recipes are designed to fuel your body in a way that promotes optimal metabolic health, reduces inflammation, and provides sustained, balanced energy throughout your day.

When I first started cooking with these principles in mind, I noticed a profound difference—not just in how I felt physically, but also in my mental clarity and overall well-being. The idea is simple: when we give our bodies what they need at a cellular level, everything works better. From the meals that kickstart your day to the snacks that keep you going and the dinners that bring you comfort, each recipe in this book is built on the foundation of whole foods, healthy fats, and nutrient-dense ingredients.

But this isn't just about food. It's about a lifestyle. It's about understanding how everything we consume impacts our energy levels and, ultimately, our quality of life. Whether you're a seasoned cook or just getting started, these recipes are meant to be approachable and enjoyable. I've crafted each one with the same love and attention I would for my own family, keeping in mind that what we eat should not only be good for us but also bring joy to our lives.

So, let's get cooking, and let's start fueling ourselves with the kind of energy that helps us live our best lives every day.

Grab your apron, sharpen your knives, and get ready to cook with purpose. Together, we'll explore the endless possibilities of Good Energy Cooking and discover how food can be your most powerful tool for a vibrant, energetic life.

Here's to cooking with love, intention, and the best energy possible. Let's get started!

How to Use This Cookbook

This cookbook is your guide to embracing the Good Energy philosophy in your everyday life. Whether you're new to this way of eating or already familiar with its benefits, I've designed these recipes to be approachable, practical, and—most importantly—delicious.

1. Start with the Basics: If you're new to the Good Energy principles, begin with some of the simpler recipes. These will introduce you to the key ingredients and flavors that define this way of eating. As you get more comfortable, you can move on to more complex dishes.

2. Customize to Your Needs: Everyone's body is different, and what works for one person might not work for another. Feel free to adapt the recipes to suit your tastes and dietary needs. The beauty of cooking at home is that you can control what goes into your food, making it easier to align with your personal health goals.

3. Plan Your Meals: I've organized the recipes into categories—breakfast, lunch, dinner, snacks, appetizers, desserts, and drinks—to help you plan your meals throughout the day. This makes it easy to ensure that you're eating a balanced diet that supports good energy levels from morning till night.

4. Focus on Quality: Whenever possible, choose the highest quality ingredients you can find. Organic produce, grass-fed meats, wild-caught fish, and minimally processed foods are all great choices that align with the Good Energy philosophy.

5. Enjoy the Process: Cooking should be a joy, not a chore. Take your time, enjoy the aromas, the textures, and the satisfaction that comes from creating something nourishing for yourself and your loved ones. Remember, the energy you put into your cooking is just as important as the energy you get out of it.

How This Cookbook Can Help You

This cookbook is more than just a collection of recipes; it's a guide to transforming the way you eat, think, and feel. Rooted in the principles of Good Energy as taught by Dr. Casey Means, every recipe here is designed to support your metabolic health, boost your energy levels, and help you feel your best every day.

Here's how this cookbook can help you:

1. **Optimize Your Metabolism:** Every recipe in this book is crafted to support your metabolic health. By focusing on nutrient-dense, anti-inflammatory ingredients, you'll be giving your body the tools it needs to create and sustain good energy, helping you to feel more vibrant and alive.
2. **Simplify Healthy Eating:** I've taken the guesswork out of healthy eating by creating meals that are balanced, easy to prepare, and delicious. Whether you're a seasoned chef or just starting out in the kitchen, these recipes are straightforward and accessible, making it easier to stick to your health goals.
3. **Adapt to Your Lifestyle:** Life can be busy, and maintaining a healthy diet often feels like a challenge. This cookbook offers practical tips for meal prep, planning, and shopping, so you can easily integrate these recipes into your daily routine without stress or overwhelm.
4. **Enjoy Delicious Food:** Eating well doesn't mean sacrificing flavor. These recipes are designed to be both nourishing and satisfying, proving that healthy food can be incredibly delicious. You'll find yourself looking forward to every meal, knowing that it's not only good for you but tastes great too.
5. **Empower Your Health Journey:** This cookbook empowers you to take control of your health by providing the knowledge and tools you need to make informed choices. With the principles of Good Energy guiding you, you'll gain confidence in the kitchen and in your ability to nourish yourself and your loved ones.

The Good Energy Philosophy

When it comes to food, I've always believed that what we eat has a direct impact on how we feel. But it wasn't until I started diving into the principles laid out by Dr. Casey Means in Good Energy: The Surprising Connection Between Metabolism and Limitless Health that I truly understood the depth of that connection. The Good Energy philosophy is all about fueling your body in a way that supports optimal metabolic health, reduces inflammation, and gives you steady, lasting energy.

What does that mean in practical terms? It means focusing on whole, unprocessed foods—ingredients that are as close to their natural state as possible. We're talking about vibrant vegetables, high-quality proteins, healthy fats, and foods rich in fiber and antioxidants. It's about embracing ingredients that nourish not just your body, but your mind and spirit too.

I've spent countless hours experimenting with these principles in my own kitchen, and the results have been nothing short of life-changing. I've found that when I choose foods that support my metabolism, I feel more energized, more focused, and just plain better. And the best part? These foods are delicious. You don't have to sacrifice flavor to eat in a way that supports your health.

So, the Good Energy philosophy is really about making choices that benefit your whole being. It's about understanding that every meal is an opportunity to take care of yourself, to feed your body with what it needs to thrive. And once you start doing that, you'll be amazed at how much better you feel—physically, mentally, and emotionally.

The Importance of Metabolic Health in Everyday Cooking

When I first started focusing on metabolic health in my cooking, it was like a light bulb went off in my head. I realized that what we eat does so much more than just fill us up—it has a profound impact on how our bodies function, how we feel, and even how we think. It's about giving our bodies the right kind of fuel to keep everything running smoothly, from our energy levels to our mood and overall well-being.

Metabolic health is all about how efficiently your body converts food into energy. When your metabolism is working well, you feel energized, your mind is clear, and you're more resilient to stress. But when it's out of balance—often because of poor food choices—it can lead to fatigue, brain fog, and a host of other health issues.

That's why I'm so passionate about incorporating the principles of metabolic health into everyday cooking. It's not about following some strict diet or depriving yourself of foods you love. Instead, it's about making simple, thoughtful choices that support your metabolism, like using whole, unprocessed ingredients, balancing your macronutrients, and paying attention to how different foods make you feel.

In my own kitchen, I've seen firsthand how making small changes can lead to big improvements in how I feel. For instance, swapping out refined carbs for whole grains, adding more leafy greens to my meals, or choosing healthy fats like avocado or olive oil can make a world of difference. It's these little tweaks that help keep my metabolism humming along, giving me steady energy throughout the day.

And here's the best part—cooking with metabolic health in mind doesn't mean sacrificing flavor. In fact, the recipes in this cookbook are packed with vibrant, satisfying flavors that will make you forget you're even thinking about health. It's about finding that sweet spot where delicious food meets powerful nutrition.

Understanding Good Energy

Let's talk about Good Energy. What exactly does it mean? To me, Good Energy is about feeling your best every single day, and it all starts with what you put on your plate. The concept, as Dr. Casey Means explains in her book, revolves around fueling your body in a way that supports optimal metabolic function, reduces inflammation, and keeps your energy levels steady and consistent.

I think of Good Energy as that feeling when you wake up refreshed, power through your day with a clear mind, and still have enough energy left to enjoy the evening. It's not about quick bursts of energy followed by crashes; it's about sustaining a level of vitality that carries you through whatever life throws your way.

In my experience, achieving Good Energy is all about balance—balancing your meals with the right mix of nutrients, balancing your life with proper rest and activity, and even balancing your mind with mindfulness and stress management. It's all connected.

The recipes you'll find in this cookbook are designed with these principles in mind. They're crafted to provide you with the nutrients your body needs to maintain that Good Energy throughout the day. Whether it's a hearty breakfast that fuels your morning, a balanced lunch that keeps you going, or a dinner that helps you wind down without feeling sluggish, every recipe is a step toward better metabolic health and, ultimately, better energy.

As you cook your way through these pages, I encourage you to pay attention to how you feel. Notice the difference in your energy levels, your mood, and even your sleep. That's the power of Good Energy in action. And once you start experiencing it for yourself, you'll never want to go back.

Key Principles of Good Energy Eating

When it comes to eating for Good Energy, there are a few key principles that I always keep in mind. These aren't complicated rules but more like guiding lights that help me make choices in the kitchen that fuel both my body and mind. After years of trial and error, I've found that sticking to these principles not only keeps my energy levels steady but also makes cooking and eating a whole lot more enjoyable.

1. Focus on Whole, Unprocessed Foods

One of the first things I learned is that whole, unprocessed foods are the foundation of Good Energy eating. When you choose ingredients in their most natural state—think fresh vegetables, fruits, whole grains, nuts, seeds, and high-quality proteins—you're giving your body the nutrients it needs without all the additives that can drag your energy down. I always try to fill my kitchen with these kinds of foods, because they're the building blocks of meals that truly nourish.

2. Balance Your Macronutrients

Another important principle is balancing your macronutrients—carbohydrates, proteins, and fats. Each of these plays a vital role in how your body functions, and getting the right mix can help keep your energy steady throughout the day. For example, when I'm putting together a meal, I make sure it includes a good source of protein (like eggs, fish, or legumes), healthy fats (like avocado or olive oil), and complex carbohydrates (like quinoa or sweet potatoes). This combination helps avoid energy spikes and crashes, keeping you fueled and satisfied.

3. Prioritize Anti-Inflammatory Ingredients

Inflammation is a big energy zapper, so I always aim to include anti-inflammatory ingredients in my meals. Foods like leafy greens, berries, turmeric, and fatty fish are not only delicious but also help reduce inflammation in the body. I've noticed that when I regularly include these foods in my diet, I feel more energized and less sluggish.

4. Hydration is Key

Don't underestimate the power of hydration. Staying well-hydrated is essential for maintaining Good Energy. I always keep a water bottle nearby and try to include hydrating foods like cucumbers, watermelon, and leafy greens in my meals. If you're looking for a little extra flavor, herbal teas or water infused with fruits and herbs are great options.

5. Listen to Your Body

Lastly, and perhaps most importantly, listen to your body. It's easy to get caught up in what we "should" be eating, but I've found that tuning into how different foods make me feel is the best guide. If something doesn't sit right or leaves you feeling drained, it's okay to adjust. Good Energy is all about finding what works best for you, and that can take some experimenting.

Tips for Stocking a Good Energy Kitchen

Having the right ingredients on hand is half the battle when it comes to cooking for Good Energy. I like to think of my kitchen as my toolbox—if it's well-stocked, I'm always ready to whip up something that's both nourishing and delicious. Here are some tips I've picked up over the years to keep your kitchen ready for Good Energy cooking.

1. Keep Your Pantry Full of Basics

First things first, make sure you have a good selection of pantry staples. These are the items that you'll turn to again and again, so it's worth investing in quality. I always keep a variety of whole grains like quinoa, brown rice, and oats on hand, along with beans and lentils for plant-based proteins. Nuts, seeds, and dried fruits are great for snacks and adding texture to dishes. And don't forget healthy oils like extra virgin olive oil and coconut oil—they're essential for cooking and dressing salads.

2. Fresh Produce is Your Best Friend

When it comes to fresh produce, I like to stock up on a mix of leafy greens, colorful vegetables, and fruits. Leafy greens like spinach, kale, and arugula are incredibly versatile—you can toss them in a salad, blend them into a smoothie, or sauté them as a side. I also make sure to have a good selection of seasonal veggies and fruits. They're not only more flavorful but also pack the most nutrients.

3. Don't Forget Your Protein Sources

Whether you're plant-based or eat animal products, having a variety of protein sources in your kitchen is key. For me, that means having eggs, fish, and organic poultry in the fridge, along with a stock of beans, lentils, tofu, and tempeh in the pantry. These are the building blocks of satisfying meals that keep you full and energized.

4. Stock Up on Flavor Enhancers

Herbs, spices, and condiments are what make healthy cooking exciting. I always have a range of herbs and spices on hand—turmeric, cumin, garlic powder, and fresh herbs like basil and cilantro are some of my go-tos. These not only add flavor but also come with their own health benefits. I also keep things like apple cider vinegar, tamari (a gluten-free soy sauce alternative), and a good-quality mustard for quick and tasty dressings and marinades.

5. Prep for Success

One thing that really helps me stay on track is doing a bit of prep work ahead of time. I like to chop vegetables, cook a big batch of quinoa or brown rice, and roast some sweet potatoes at the beginning of the week. Having these ready to go makes it so much easier to throw together a meal when life gets busy. Trust me, a little prep goes a long way in keeping your Good Energy kitchen running smoothly.

With these tips, you'll be well on your way to stocking a kitchen that's ready to support your journey toward better energy, health, and overall well-being. Remember, it's all about making small, sustainable changes that fit your lifestyle. Happy cooking!

Lifestyle Tips for Good Energy

Living with Good Energy isn't just about what you eat—though that's a huge part of it. It's also about how you live your life day to day. Over the years, I've learned that small, consistent habits can make a big difference in how I feel, both physically and mentally. Here are some lifestyle tips that I've found help me stay energized, focused, and balanced, all rooted in the principles of Good Energy.

1. Prioritize Sleep

I can't stress enough how important sleep is for maintaining Good Energy. When I don't get enough sleep, everything else suffers—my mood, my focus, and even my food choices. I aim for 7-8 hours of quality sleep every night, making my bedroom a calm and comfortable space. I also try to stick to a consistent sleep schedule, going to bed and waking up at the same time every day, even on weekends. Trust me, when you're well-rested, everything else falls into place more easily.

2. Stay Active—But Find What You Love

Exercise is a crucial part of keeping my energy levels steady, but it doesn't have to mean hitting the gym every day. I've found that the key is to find activities that I genuinely enjoy. For me, that's a mix of yoga, hiking, and the occasional dance class. Moving my body every day, even if it's just a short walk, keeps my metabolism humming and helps clear my mind. The best exercise is the one you actually look forward to doing, so experiment until you find what works for you.

3. Manage Stress Mindfully

Stress is a big energy drain, and it's something we all deal with. Over time, I've learned some techniques that help me manage stress in a way that supports my Good Energy. Meditation and deep breathing exercises are part of my daily routine, even if it's just for a few minutes in the morning or before bed. I also make time for things that bring me joy and relaxation, whether that's reading a book, spending time with loved ones, or simply sitting in the sun with a cup of tea.

4. Hydrate Like You Mean It

It's easy to overlook, but staying hydrated is fundamental to feeling good. I always keep a water bottle nearby and sip throughout the day. I also like to add a slice of lemon or cucumber to my water for a little extra flavor and a boost of antioxidants. Proper hydration helps keep your energy levels stable, supports digestion, and even improves your skin. It's such a simple habit, but it makes a world of difference.

5. Embrace Mindful Eating

One of the biggest shifts I've made is to approach eating as an experience, not just something I do on autopilot. I try to eat mindfully, savoring each bite and paying attention to how my body feels. This not only enhances the enjoyment of my meals but also helps me tune into my body's hunger and fullness cues. When I eat with intention, I find that I'm more satisfied and energized by my food.

6. Cultivate a Supportive Environment

Who you surround yourself with can have a big impact on your energy and overall well-being. I make it a point to nurture relationships that uplift and support me. Whether it's family, friends, or a community group, having a strong support system makes living a Good Energy lifestyle more sustainable and enjoyable. I also try to keep my home environment clutter-free and filled with things that inspire and calm me.

BREAKFAST RECIPES

Quinoa Breakfast Bowl with Blueberries and Almond Butter

Gluten-Free, Dairy-Free, Soy-Free

I love starting my day with this Quinoa Breakfast Bowl because it's packed with protein, fiber, and healthy fats to keep me full and energized all morning. It's quick to make and absolutely delicious, with the perfect mix of flavors and textures. I'm sure you'll enjoy it just as much as I do!

Prep time: 5 minutes | Cooking time: 15 minutes | Servings: 2

Ingredients:

- 1/2 cup quinoa, rinsed
- 1 cup water
- 1/4 teaspoon sea salt
- 1/2 teaspoon ground cinnamon
- 1/2 teaspoon vanilla extract
- 1/2 cup fresh blueberries

- 2 tablespoons almond butter (unsweetened)
- 1 tablespoon chia seeds
- 1 tablespoon hemp seeds
- 1 tablespoon unsweetened shredded coconut
- 1/2 cup unsweetened almond milk

Step-by-Step Directions:

1. Cook the Quinoa: I always start by rinsing the quinoa under cold water to remove any bitterness. Then, I combine the quinoa with 1 cup of water and a pinch of sea salt in a small saucepan. Bring it to a boil over medium heat, then lower the heat, cover the pan, and let it simmer for about 15 minutes. You'll know it's done when the water is absorbed, and the quinoa is tender.
2. Add Flavor: Once the quinoa is cooked, I stir in the cinnamon and vanilla extract. This gives it a lovely warm flavor that pairs so well with the rest of the ingredients.
3. Assemble Your Bowl: Now, I divide the quinoa between two bowls. On top of each, I add the fresh blueberries, a dollop of almond butter, chia seeds, hemp seeds, and a sprinkle of shredded coconut. For a creamier texture, I pour a little almond milk over the top.
4. Enjoy Your Creation: That's it! You've made a Quinoa Breakfast Bowl that's not only tasty but also nourishing. Sit back and enjoy this hearty, energizing meal.

Nutritional Information (Per Serving):

- Calories: 340 | Protein: 10g | Fiber: 9g | Healthy Fats: 18g | Carbs: 38g

Tips:

1. Make Ahead: I often cook extra quinoa and keep it in the fridge for a couple of days. This way, I can quickly put together a breakfast bowl in the morning.
2. Switch It Up: Feel free to swap out the blueberries for other fruits like strawberries or raspberries if you prefer.

Zucchini and Sweet Potato Hash with Poached Eggs

Gluten-Free, Soy-Free, Nut-Free

I love making this Zucchini and Sweet Potato Hash with Poached Eggs when I want a breakfast that's both filling and packed with nutrients. The combination of sweet potatoes and zucchini offers a balance of complex carbs and fiber, while the poached eggs add a rich source of protein to keep you energized. This dish is not only delicious but also supports metabolic health, thanks to its anti-inflammatory ingredients and balanced nutrition. It's a great way to start your day feeling satisfied and ready to take on anything.

Prep time: 10 minutes | Cooking time: 20 minutes | Servings: 2

Ingredients:

- 1 medium sweet potato, peeled and diced into 1/2-inch cubes
- 1 medium zucchini, diced into 1/2-inch cubes
- 1 small red onion, finely chopped
- 1 red bell pepper, diced
- 2 tablespoons extra-virgin olive oil
- 1/2 teaspoon sea salt, plus more to taste
- 1/4 teaspoon freshly ground black pepper
- 1/2 teaspoon smoked paprika
- 1/2 teaspoon ground cumin
- 4 large eggs (pasture-raised, if possible)
- 1 tablespoon white vinegar (for poaching the eggs)
- 1 tablespoon chopped fresh parsley (for garnish)

Step-by-Step Directions:

1. Prepare the Hash: I start by heating 1 tablespoon of olive oil in a large skillet over medium heat. Once the oil is hot, I add the diced sweet potatoes and cook them for about 8-10 minutes, stirring occasionally, until they begin to soften and turn golden brown.
2. Add the Veggies: Next, I add the chopped red onion, red bell pepper, and zucchini to the skillet. I season everything with sea salt, black pepper, smoked paprika, and ground cumin. I continue to cook the mixture for another 8-10 minutes, stirring occasionally, until the vegetables are tender and the flavors are well combined.
3. Poach the Eggs: While the hash is finishing up, I bring a medium pot of water to a gentle simmer. I add 1 tablespoon of white vinegar to the water—this helps the egg whites hold together. I crack each egg into a small bowl, then gently slide the eggs into the simmering water one at a time. I let them cook for about 3-4 minutes, until the whites are set but the yolks are still soft. Using a slotted spoon, I carefully remove the eggs from the water and place them on a paper towel to drain.
4. Assemble the Dish: I divide the hash between two plates and top each with two poached eggs. I like to finish it off with a sprinkle of fresh parsley for a burst of color and flavor.
5. Enjoy: Your Zucchini and Sweet Potato Hash with Poached Eggs is ready to enjoy! The combination of flavors and textures makes this a satisfying and nutrient-packed breakfast.

Nutritional Information (Per Serving):

- Calories: 350 | Protein: 14g | Fiber: 6g | Healthy Fats: 20g | Carbs: 30g

Tips:

1. Cook Ahead: You can make the hash ahead of time and reheat it quickly in a skillet. Just add the freshly poached eggs when you're ready to serve.
2. Spice It Up: If you like a bit of heat, try adding a pinch of red pepper flakes to the hash while cooking.

Serving Suggestions:

- This dish pairs beautifully with a simple side of mixed greens or a fresh fruit salad. I often enjoy it with a cup of herbal tea or a refreshing glass of lemon water.

Coconut and Flaxseed Pancakes with Warm Berry Compote

Gluten-Free, Dairy-Free, Soy-Free

These are one of my favorite ways to start the day. They're light, fluffy, and packed with nutrients that keep me energized all morning. The combination of coconut and flaxseeds provides healthy fats and fiber, while the warm berry compote adds a touch of natural sweetness and antioxidants. This breakfast not only tastes amazing but also supports metabolic health and balanced nutrition, aligning perfectly with the Good Energy principles.

Prep time: 10 minutes | Cooking time: 20 minutes | Servings: 2

Ingredients:

- For the Pancakes:
- 1/2 cup coconut flour
- 2 tablespoons ground flaxseeds
- 1/2 teaspoon baking powder
- 1/4 teaspoon sea salt
- 1/2 teaspoon ground cinnamon
- 4 large eggs
- 1/2 cup unsweetened almond milk (or any Good Energy-approved nut milk)
- 1 tablespoon maple syrup (optional, for a touch of sweetness)
- 1 teaspoon vanilla extract
- 2 tablespoons coconut oil (for cooking)
- For the Warm Berry Compote:
- 1 cup mixed berries (fresh or frozen)
- 1 tablespoon lemon juice
- 1 tablespoon maple syrup (optional)
- 1/2 teaspoon vanilla extract

Step-by-Step Directions:

1. Prepare the Pancake Batter: I start by whisking together the coconut flour, ground flaxseeds, baking powder, sea salt, and ground cinnamon in a large mixing bowl. In a separate bowl, I beat the eggs and then add the almond milk, maple syrup (if using), and vanilla extract. I gradually mix the wet ingredients into the dry ingredients until everything is well combined and the batter is smooth.
2. Cook the Pancakes: I heat a tablespoon of coconut oil in a large non-stick skillet over medium heat. Once the oil is hot, I pour about 1/4 cup of batter into the skillet for each pancake. I cook the pancakes for about 2-3 minutes on each side, or until they're golden brown and cooked through. You'll know it's time to flip when bubbles start to form on the surface of the pancakes. Repeat with the remaining batter, adding more coconut oil to the skillet as needed.
3. Make the Warm Berry Compote: While the pancakes are cooking, I prepare the berry compote. I place the mixed berries, lemon juice, maple syrup (if using), and vanilla extract in a small saucepan over medium heat. I cook the mixture for about 5 minutes, stirring occasionally, until the berries break down and the compote thickens slightly.
4. Serve the Pancakes: I stack the pancakes on two plates and spoon the warm berry compote over the top. The combination of flavors is absolutely delicious, and the compote adds just the right amount of natural sweetness.
5. Enjoy: These pancakes are best enjoyed right away while they're still warm. The light texture and rich flavors make them a wonderful start to any morning.

Nutritional Information (Per Serving):

- Calories: 380 | Protein: 12g | Fiber: 10g | Healthy Fats: 28g | Carbs: 28g

Tips:

1. Keep Them Warm: If you're making a larger batch, you can keep the cooked pancakes warm in a 200°F oven while you finish cooking the rest.
2. Berry Options: Feel free to use any combination of berries you like for the compote, such as strawberries, raspberries, or blueberries.

Smoked Salmon and Avocado Omelette

Gluten-Free, Soy-Free, Nut-Free

When I'm looking for a breakfast that's both delicious and packed with nutrients, this Smoked Salmon and Avocado Omelette is my go-to. The combination of omega-3-rich smoked salmon, creamy avocado, and fresh herbs makes this omelette not only tasty but also incredibly nourishing. It's perfect for supporting metabolic health and provides balanced nutrition to start your day strong.

Prep time: 5 minutes | Cooking time: 10 minutes | Servings: 1

Ingredients:

- 3 large eggs (pasture-raised, if possible)
- 1/4 teaspoon sea salt
- 1/4 teaspoon freshly ground black pepper
- 1 tablespoon extra-virgin olive oil (or ghee for cooking)
- 2 ounces smoked salmon, sliced into small pieces
- 1/2 avocado, sliced
- 1 tablespoon chopped fresh dill
- 1 tablespoon chopped fresh chives
- 1/4 teaspoon lemon zest (optional, for a fresh flavor)
- Lemon wedge (for serving)

Step-by-Step Directions:

1. Prepare the Egg Mixture: I like to start by cracking the eggs into a small bowl and whisking them together with the sea salt and black pepper. This ensures the eggs are well-seasoned and the omelette turns out fluffy.
2. Cook the Omelette: Heat a non-stick skillet over medium heat and add the olive oil or ghee. Once the oil is hot, I pour in the egg mixture, tilting the pan to ensure the eggs spread out evenly. As the eggs start to set around the edges (after about 1-2 minutes), I gently lift the edges with a spatula to let the uncooked eggs flow underneath.
3. Add the Fillings: When the eggs are mostly set but still slightly runny on top, I evenly distribute the smoked salmon pieces, avocado slices, dill, and chives over one half of the omelette. The combination of these ingredients not only adds amazing flavor but also provides a great mix of healthy fats and protein.
4. Fold and Finish: Using a spatula, I carefully fold the omelette in half to cover the fillings. I let it cook for another minute or so until the inside is cooked through but still soft and creamy.
5. I slide the omelette onto a plate and garnish it with a sprinkle of fresh herbs and a touch of lemon zest for an extra burst of flavor. A lemon wedge on the side adds a refreshing touch if you like a bit of acidity.

Nutritional Information (Per Serving):

- Calories: 370 | Protein: 20g | Fiber: 4g | Healthy Fats: 30g | Carbs: 5g

Tips:

1. Make It Your Own: If you enjoy a bit more spice, you can add a dash of hot sauce or a sprinkle of red pepper flakes to the egg mixture.
2. Avoid Overcooking: To keep the omelette soft and fluffy, be careful not to overcook the eggs—remove from the heat just as the eggs finish setting.

Serving Suggestions:

- This omelette pairs beautifully with a simple side salad of mixed greens tossed with lemon and olive oil, or you can enjoy it with a slice of gluten-free toast. A cup of green tea or a fresh smoothie makes for a perfect morning beverage.

Collard Green Breakfast Wraps with Turkey Sausage

Gluten-Free, Dairy-Free, Soy-Free, Nut-Free

I love these Collard Green Breakfast Wraps because they're loaded with lean protein, healthy fats, and vibrant veggies. The turkey sausage provides a great source of protein, while the collard greens are rich in vitamins and fiber, making them a fantastic alternative to traditional wraps. The combination of nutrient-dense ingredients helps me stay full and energized throughout the morning. Plus, these wraps are quick to make and easy to customize, so they're perfect for a nutritious, on-the-go breakfast.

Prep time: 10 minutes | Cooking time: 15 minutes | Servings: 2 wraps

Ingredients:

- 4 large collard green leaves, stems trimmed
- 2 turkey sausages (choose a clean, Good Energy-approved brand with no added sugars or preservatives)
- 2 large eggs
- 1/2 avocado, sliced
- 1/2 cup cherry tomatoes, halved
- 1 tablespoon extra-virgin olive oil
- 1/4 teaspoon sea salt
- 1/4 teaspoon black pepper
- 1 tablespoon chopped fresh parsley (optional, for garnish)
- Lemon wedges, for serving

Step-by-Step Directions:

1. Prep the Collard Greens: I start by trimming the thick stems from the collard green leaves so they're easier to fold. Then, I blanch them for about 30 seconds in boiling water, just until they soften up. After blanching, I immediately transfer the leaves to a bowl of ice water to stop the cooking process. Pat them dry with a clean towel and set them aside.
2. Cook the Turkey Sausage: I heat 1 tablespoon of olive oil in a skillet over medium heat. I add the turkey sausages and cook them for about 8-10 minutes, turning occasionally, until they're browned and cooked through. Once they're done, I remove them from the pan and slice them into bite-sized pieces.
3. Scramble the Eggs: In the same skillet, I crack the eggs and season them with sea salt and black pepper. I scramble them gently over medium heat, stirring occasionally until the eggs are just set but still soft. This takes about 2-3 minutes.
4. Assemble the Wraps: Now, I lay out the collard green leaves flat on a clean surface. I layer the scrambled eggs, turkey sausage slices, avocado, and cherry tomatoes evenly onto the center of each leaf. Then, I fold in the sides of the collard greens and roll them up tightly like a burrito.
5. Serve: Once the wraps are assembled, I garnish them with fresh parsley if I'm feeling fancy, and serve them with lemon wedges on the side for a refreshing zing. These wraps are best enjoyed fresh, but you can also wrap them tightly in foil for a portable breakfast.

Nutritional Information (Per Serving):

- Calories: 360 | Protein: 24g | Fiber: 8g | Healthy Fats: 25g | Carbs: 12g

Tips:

1. Blanching Tip: Blanching the collard greens helps make them more pliable for rolling without tearing.
2. Meal Prep: These wraps are easy to prep ahead of time. You can store the components separately and quickly assemble them in the morning.

Sweet Potato and Spinach Breakfast Hash

Gluten-Free, Soy-Free, Nut-Free

This Sweet Potato and Spinach Breakfast Hash is one of my favorite ways to start the day because it's packed with nutrients and flavors that keep me full and energized. Sweet potatoes provide complex carbs and fiber, while spinach adds a boost of vitamins and minerals. The combination of these ingredients supports metabolic health and provides a balanced, anti-inflammatory breakfast that's easy to make and delicious to eat.

Prep time: 10 minutes | Cooking time: 20 minutes | Servings: 2

Ingredients:

- 1 medium sweet potato, peeled and diced into 1/2-inch cubes
- 1 small red onion, finely chopped
- 1 red bell pepper, diced
- 2 cloves garlic, minced
- 2 tablespoons extra-virgin olive oil
- 1 teaspoon smoked paprika
- 1/2 teaspoon ground cumin
- 1/4 teaspoon sea salt, or to taste
- 1/4 teaspoon black pepper, or to taste
- 2 cups fresh spinach, loosely packed
- 2 large eggs (optional, for added protein)
- Fresh parsley, chopped, for garnish (optional)

Step-by-Step Directions:

1. Prepare the Sweet Potatoes: I start by heating 1 tablespoon of olive oil in a large skillet over medium heat. Once the oil is hot, I add the diced sweet potatoes and cook them for about 10 minutes, stirring occasionally, until they start to soften and turn golden brown.
2. Add the Veggies: Next, I add the chopped red onion, red bell pepper, and minced garlic to the skillet with the sweet potatoes. I season everything with smoked paprika, ground cumin, sea salt, and black pepper. I cook the mixture for another 8-10 minutes, stirring occasionally, until the vegetables are tender and nicely browned.
3. Add the Spinach: Once the veggies are cooked, I stir in the fresh spinach and cook for another 2-3 minutes, just until the spinach wilts down. This adds a vibrant color and loads of nutrients to the dish.
4. Optional: Add the Eggs: If I'm in the mood for extra protein, I make a little well in the hash and crack an egg into it. I cover the skillet and let the egg cook for about 3-4 minutes, or until the egg whites are set and the yolks are still runny. You can cook the eggs longer if you prefer them fully set.
5. Serve: I divide the hash between two plates and garnish with a sprinkle of fresh parsley for a pop of color and flavor. It's ready to enjoy!

Nutritional Information (Per Serving without Eggs):

- Calories: 260 | Protein: 4g | Fiber: 7g | Healthy Fats: 14g | Carbs: 30g

Nutritional Information (Per Serving with Eggs):

- Calories: 330 | Protein: 10g | Fiber: 7g | Healthy Fats: 20g | Carbs: 30g

Tips:

1. Make It Your Own: Feel free to add other veggies you love, like mushrooms or zucchini, to the hash. They'll cook up nicely with the sweet potatoes.
2. Crisp It Up: For extra crispy sweet potatoes, cook them in a single layer without stirring too much. This allows them to get that nice golden crust.

Coconut Yogurt with Fresh Berries and Hemp Seeds

Gluten-Free, Dairy-Free, Soy-Free

When I'm short on time but still want a nourishing and delicious breakfast, this Coconut Yogurt with Fresh Berries and Hemp Seeds is my go-to. It's quick, easy, and packed with nutrients that support metabolic health. The coconut yogurt provides a creamy base rich in healthy fats, while the fresh berries add a burst of antioxidants. Hemp seeds offer a boost of plant-based protein and omega-3 fatty acids, making this breakfast both satisfying and energizing.

Prep time: 5 minutes | Cooking time: None | Servings: 1

Ingredients:

- 1 cup coconut yogurt (unsweetened)
- 1/2 cup mixed fresh berries (such as blueberries, strawberries, raspberries)
- 1 tablespoon hemp seeds
- 1 teaspoon chia seeds (optional, for added fiber)
- 1 teaspoon raw honey or maple syrup (optional, for sweetness)
- 1/2 teaspoon vanilla extract (optional, for flavor)
- 1 tablespoon unsweetened shredded coconut (optional, for texture)

Step-by-Step Directions:

1. Prepare the Yogurt Base: I like to start by spooning the coconut yogurt into a serving bowl. If you want to add a touch of sweetness, stir in the raw honey or maple syrup and vanilla extract until well combined. This gives the yogurt a light sweetness and extra flavor.
2. Add the Toppings: Next, I top the yogurt with a generous handful of mixed fresh berries. The berries not only add a beautiful pop of color but are also loaded with antioxidants that help combat inflammation.
3. Sprinkle the Seeds: I then sprinkle the hemp seeds and chia seeds over the berries. These seeds provide a great source of protein, fiber, and omega-3 fatty acids, which are fantastic for keeping you full and supporting brain health.
4. Finish with Coconut: If you like a bit of texture, sprinkle some unsweetened shredded coconut over the top. It adds a nice crunch and enhances the coconut flavor of the yogurt.
5. Enjoy: Your Coconut Yogurt with Fresh Berries and Hemp Seeds is ready to enjoy! It's perfect for a quick breakfast that's both delicious and packed with nutrients.

Nutritional Information (Per Serving):

- Calories: 250 | Protein: 6g | Fiber: 7g | Healthy Fats: 18g | Carbs: 18g

Tips:

1. Make It Your Own: Feel free to switch up the berries based on what's in season or what you have on hand. You can also add a sprinkle of nuts like almonds or walnuts for extra crunch.
2. Meal Prep: You can prepare the yogurt base and toppings separately in advance, and simply combine them in the morning for an even quicker breakfast.

Serving Suggestions:

- This breakfast is perfect on its own, but I sometimes like to pair it with a warm cup of green tea or a refreshing glass of lemon water. If you're feeling extra hungry, you can serve it with a slice of gluten-free toast topped with almond butter.

Almond Butter and Banana Smoothie

Gluten-Free, Dairy-Free, Soy-Free

This Almond Butter and Banana Smoothie is one of my favorite quick breakfasts when I'm in the mood for something creamy and satisfying. It's loaded with healthy fats, fiber, and natural sweetness, which keep me energized and full throughout the morning. The combination of almond butter and banana not only tastes delicious but also supports metabolic health and provides balanced nutrition. It's an easy way to start your day with a nutrient-packed meal that aligns perfectly with the Good Energy principles.

Prep time: 5 minutes | Cooking time: None | Servings: 1

Ingredients:

- 1 ripe banana, frozen for a creamier texture
- 2 tablespoons almond butter (unsweetened, no added oils or sugars)
- 1/2 cup unsweetened almond milk (or any Good Energy-approved nut milk)
- 1 tablespoon ground flaxseeds (for added fiber and omega-3s)
- 1/2 teaspoon ground cinnamon (for its anti-inflammatory properties)
- 1 teaspoon vanilla extract (optional, for extra flavor)
- 1/4 cup ice cubes (optional, for a thicker smoothie)
- 1 tablespoon hemp seeds (optional, for extra protein and healthy fats)

Step-by-Step Directions:

1. Prepare the Ingredients: I like to start by gathering all the ingredients. If your banana isn't already frozen, you can use a fresh one, but freezing it beforehand gives the smoothie a thicker, creamier texture.
2. Blend Everything Together: In a high-speed blender, I combine the frozen banana, almond butter, unsweetened almond milk, ground flaxseeds, ground cinnamon, and vanilla extract. If you want a thicker smoothie, add a few ice cubes. Blend on high speed for about 30 seconds, or until everything is smooth and creamy.
3. Adjust Consistency: If the smoothie is too thick, you can add a bit more almond milk until you reach your desired consistency. I like mine to be just thick enough to sip slowly and savor every bit.
4. Serve: Pour the smoothie into a glass. If you're using hemp seeds, sprinkle them on top for a little extra crunch and a boost of protein.
5. Enjoy: This smoothie is best enjoyed immediately while it's still cold and refreshing. It's a perfect way to fuel your morning with a balanced, nutrient-rich breakfast.

Nutritional Information (Per Serving):

- Calories: 350 | Protein: 8g | Fiber: 7g | Healthy Fats: 22g | Carbs: 32g

Tips:

1. Prep Ahead: You can prepare the ingredients the night before and store them in the fridge or freezer, so all you have to do in the morning is blend and go.
2. Boost It: For an extra protein boost, you can add a scoop of plant-based protein powder. This is especially great if you're having this smoothie after a workout.

Serving Suggestions:

- This smoothie is a complete meal on its own, but you can pair it with a handful of nuts or a slice of gluten-free toast if you're extra hungry. It's also a great base for adding your favorite superfoods, like a spoonful of chia seeds or a dash of turmeric.

Quinoa Porridge with Cinnamon and Walnuts

Gluten-Free, Dairy-Free, Soy-Free

When I want a warm, comforting breakfast that's also nourishing and satisfying, I turn to this Quinoa Porridge with Cinnamon and Walnuts. It's a fantastic way to start the day with a meal that's rich in protein, fiber, and healthy fats. The cinnamon adds a warm spice that's not only delicious but also supports metabolic health, while the walnuts provide a satisfying crunch and a dose of omega-3 fatty acids. This porridge is the perfect blend of flavors and textures, all while aligning with the Good Energy principles.

Prep time: 5 minutes | Cooking time: 20 minutes | Servings: 2

Ingredients:

- 1/2 cup quinoa, rinsed
- 1 cup unsweetened almond milk (or any Good Energy-approved nut milk)
- 1/2 cup water
- 1 tablespoon maple syrup (optional, for sweetness)
- 1/2 teaspoon ground cinnamon
- 1/4 teaspoon vanilla extract (optional, for flavor)
- 1/4 cup chopped walnuts
- 1 tablespoon ground flaxseeds (for added fiber and omega-3s)
- 1/4 cup fresh berries (optional, for garnish)
- Pinch of sea salt

Step-by-Step Directions:

1. Cook the Quinoa: I start by rinsing the quinoa under cold water to remove any bitterness. Then, in a medium saucepan, I combine the rinsed quinoa, almond milk, water, and a pinch of sea salt. I bring the mixture to a gentle boil over medium heat, then reduce the heat to low, cover, and let it simmer for about 15 minutes, or until the quinoa is tender and has absorbed most of the liquid.
2. Flavor the Porridge: Once the quinoa is cooked, I stir in the ground cinnamon, vanilla extract, and maple syrup (if using). The cinnamon adds warmth and depth of flavor, making the porridge feel cozy and satisfying.
3. Add the Toppings: I divide the porridge between two bowls and top each with chopped walnuts, a sprinkle of ground flaxseeds, and a handful of fresh berries. The walnuts add a nice crunch and healthy fats, while the flaxseeds boost the fiber content and provide additional omega-3s.
4. Serve and Enjoy: Your Quinoa Porridge with Cinnamon and Walnuts is ready to enjoy! It's best served warm and can be enjoyed as is, or you can add a splash of almond milk on top if you prefer a creamier texture.

Nutritional Information (Per Serving):

- Calories: 300 | Protein: 8g | Fiber: 6g | Healthy Fats: 14g | Carbs: 35g

Tips:

1. Batch Cooking: You can cook a larger batch of quinoa and store it in the fridge for up to 5 days. This way, you can quickly make porridge in the morning by reheating the quinoa with some almond milk and your favorite toppings.
2. Customizable: Feel free to customize the toppings based on what you have on hand. Sliced almonds, pumpkin seeds, or even a spoonful of almond butter would be great additions.

Serving Suggestions:

- This porridge is perfect on its own, but if you're looking for a bit more, try serving it with a side of fruit or a cup of herbal tea. It's a hearty and wholesome way to fuel your morning.

Mushroom and Kale Omelette

Gluten-Free, Soy-Free, Nut-Free

I love making this Mushroom and Kale Omelette for breakfast because it's packed with nutrients and flavors that support a healthy start to my day. The combination of mushrooms and kale provides a rich source of antioxidants, vitamins, and minerals, while the eggs offer high-quality protein. This omelette not only tastes great but also aligns perfectly with the Good Energy principles, focusing on balanced nutrition, anti-inflammatory ingredients, and metabolic health.

Prep time: 5 minutes | Cooking time: 10 minutes | Servings: 1

Ingredients:

- 2 large eggs (pasture-raised if possible)
- 1/4 cup mushrooms, sliced (any variety you prefer)
- 1/2 cup fresh kale, chopped
- 1 tablespoon extra-virgin olive oil (or ghee for cooking)
- 1/4 teaspoon sea salt
- 1/4 teaspoon black pepper
- 1/4 teaspoon garlic powder (optional, for extra flavor)
- 1 tablespoon chopped fresh parsley (optional, for garnish)

Step-by-Step Directions:

1. Prep the Ingredients: I start by cracking the eggs into a small bowl and whisking them together with sea salt, black pepper, and garlic powder if I'm using it. This gives the eggs a nice seasoning and a hint of garlic flavor that complements the mushrooms and kale.
2. Cook the Vegetables: In a non-stick skillet, I heat the olive oil over medium heat. Once the oil is hot, I add the sliced mushrooms and sauté them for about 3-4 minutes, until they start to soften and brown. Then, I add the chopped kale to the skillet, cooking it for another 2 minutes until it wilts down.
3. Cook the Omelette: I pour the beaten eggs over the mushroom and kale mixture in the skillet, tilting the pan to ensure the eggs are evenly distributed. I let the omelette cook undisturbed for about 2-3 minutes, until the edges start to set. Then, using a spatula, I carefully lift the edges and tilt the pan slightly to let any uncooked egg flow underneath.
4. Fold and Finish: Once the eggs are mostly set but still slightly soft in the center, I gently fold the omelette in half. I let it cook for another minute to ensure it's fully set but still fluffy and tender.
5. Serve: I slide the omelette onto a plate and garnish it with some freshly chopped parsley for a pop of color and added freshness. It's ready to enjoy!

Nutritional Information (Per Serving):

- Calories: 220 | Protein: 12g | Fiber: 3g | Healthy Fats: 18g | Carbs: 6g

Tips:

1. Customize It: Feel free to add other veggies like bell peppers or onions if you like. Just be sure to sauté them until tender before adding the eggs.
2. Perfect Folding: For an easier fold, use a smaller skillet so the omelette isn't too thin. This makes it easier to flip and fold without breaking.

Serving Suggestions:

- This omelette is delicious on its own, but I sometimes like to serve it with a side of sliced avocado or a small salad of mixed greens. It pairs wonderfully with a warm cup of herbal tea or a fresh green smoothie.

Buckwheat Pancakes with Blueberry Compote

Gluten-Free, Dairy-Free, Soy-Free

I love making these Buckwheat Pancakes with Blueberry Compote for breakfast because they're not only delicious but also packed with nutrients that keep me energized throughout the day. Buckwheat is naturally gluten-free and rich in fiber, which supports digestive health and helps maintain steady energy levels. The blueberry compote adds a burst of antioxidants and natural sweetness, making this breakfast both satisfying and nourishing. This recipe perfectly aligns with the Good Energy principles, focusing on metabolic health, anti-inflammatory ingredients, and balanced nutrition.

Prep time: 10 minutes | Cooking time: 20 minutes | Servings: 2

Ingredients:

- For the Buckwheat Pancakes:
- 1 cup buckwheat flour
- 1 tablespoon ground flaxseeds
- 1 teaspoon baking powder
- 1/4 teaspoon sea salt
- 1/2 teaspoon ground cinnamon
- 1 tablespoon maple syrup (optional, for sweetness)
- 1 cup unsweetened almond milk (or any Good Energy-approved nut milk)
- 1 teaspoon vanilla extract (optional, for flavor)
- 1 tablespoon coconut oil (for cooking)
- For the Blueberry Compote:
- 1 cup fresh or frozen blueberries
- 1 tablespoon lemon juice
- 1 tablespoon maple syrup (optional)
- 1/2 teaspoon vanilla extract (optional)

Step-by-Step Directions:

1. Prepare the Blueberry Compote: I start by making the blueberry compote. In a small saucepan, I combine the blueberries, lemon juice, and maple syrup (if using). I cook the mixture over medium heat, stirring occasionally, for about 5-7 minutes until the blueberries break down and the sauce thickens slightly. Once it's done, I stir in the vanilla extract and set the compote aside to cool slightly.
2. Mix the Pancake Batter: In a large mixing bowl, I whisk together the buckwheat flour, ground flaxseeds, baking powder, sea salt, and ground cinnamon. In a separate bowl, I combine the almond milk, maple syrup, and vanilla extract. I then pour the wet ingredients into the dry ingredients and mix until just combined. The batter should be slightly thick but pourable.
3. Cook the Pancakes: I heat a non-stick skillet or griddle over medium heat and add a little coconut oil to the pan. Once the oil is hot, I pour about 1/4 cup of batter onto the skillet for each pancake. I cook the pancakes for 2-3 minutes on each side, or until bubbles form on the surface and the edges look set. Then, I flip the pancakes and cook for another 2 minutes until golden brown and cooked through.
4. Serve the Pancakes: I stack the pancakes on two plates and spoon the warm blueberry compote over the top. The combination of the hearty pancakes and sweet, tangy compote is absolutely delicious.
5. Enjoy: These pancakes are best enjoyed immediately while they're still warm and fluffy. They make a wonderful breakfast that's both comforting and nourishing.

Nutritional Information (Per Serving):

- Calories: 350 | Protein: 8g | Fiber: 7g | Healthy Fats: 12g | Carbs: 55g

Tips:

1. Make It Ahead: You can prepare the blueberry compote ahead of time and store it in the fridge. Just warm it up before serving.
2. Extra Flavor: For an extra burst of flavor, you can add a pinch of nutmeg or ginger to the pancake batter.

Avocado and Spinach Smoothie Bowl

Gluten-Free, Dairy-Free, Soy-Free

This Avocado and Spinach Smoothie Bowl is one of my favorite ways to start the day because it's packed with nutrients that keep me energized and feeling great. The creamy avocado provides healthy fats, while the spinach adds a boost of vitamins and minerals. This smoothie bowl is not only delicious but also supports metabolic health and balanced nutrition, making it a perfect breakfast that aligns with the Good Energy principles.

Prep time: 5 minutes | Cooking time: None | Servings: 1

Ingredients:

- 1 ripe avocado, peeled and pitted
- 1 cup fresh spinach, tightly packed
- 1 frozen banana, sliced
- 1/2 cup frozen mango chunks
- 1/2 cup unsweetened almond milk (or any Good Energy-approved nut milk)
- 1 tablespoon chia seeds (for added fiber and omega-3s)
- 1 tablespoon hemp seeds (for extra protein and healthy fats)
- 1/2 teaspoon vanilla extract (optional, for flavor)
- 1/4 cup fresh berries (for topping)
- 1 tablespoon shredded coconut (optional, for topping)

Step-by-Step Directions:

1. Blend the Smoothie: I start by adding the avocado, spinach, frozen banana, frozen mango, almond milk, chia seeds, and vanilla extract into a high-speed blender. I blend everything on high for about 30-45 seconds until the mixture is smooth and creamy. If the smoothie is too thick, I add a little more almond milk until it reaches the consistency I like.
2. Pour and Top: Once blended, I pour the smoothie into a bowl. I like to top it with fresh berries, hemp seeds, and shredded coconut for added texture and flavor. These toppings not only make the bowl look beautiful but also provide extra nutrients.
3. Serve and Enjoy: The smoothie bowl is best enjoyed immediately while it's fresh and cold. I love how the creamy texture of the smoothie pairs with the crunch of the toppings—it's a satisfying and nutritious way to start the day.

Nutritional Information (Per Serving):

- Calories: 350 | Protein: 8g | Fiber: 12g | Healthy Fats: 22g | Carbs: 35g

Tips:

1. Customize It: Feel free to switch out the toppings based on what you have on hand. Sliced almonds, granola, or even a drizzle of almond butter would be great additions.
2. Prep Ahead: You can prepare the smoothie ingredients the night before and store them in the fridge. In the morning, just blend and go!

Serving Suggestions:

- This smoothie bowl is perfect on its own, but if you're extra hungry, you can pair it with a slice of gluten-free toast or a boiled egg for more protein. It's also great with a cup of green tea or your favorite herbal beverage.

Pumpkin-Spiced Quinoa Porridge

Gluten-Free, Dairy-Free, Soy-Free

This Pumpkin-Spiced Quinoa Porridge is a warm, comforting breakfast option that's packed with nutrients and perfect for starting your day on the right foot. It's a gluten-free, dairy-free, and soy-free dish, making it suitable for those with food sensitivities. The combination of quinoa, pumpkin, and warming spices provides a hearty meal that supports metabolic health, thanks to its balanced nutrition and anti-inflammatory ingredients.

Prep time: 5 minutes | Cooking time: 20 minutes | Servings: 2

Ingredients:

- 1/2 cup quinoa, rinsed
- 1 cup unsweetened almond milk (or any plant-based milk)
- 1/2 cup pumpkin puree (unsweetened)
- 1 tbsp maple syrup (adjust to taste)
- 1/2 tsp ground cinnamon
- 1/4 tsp ground nutmeg
- 1/4 tsp ground ginger
- 1/8 tsp ground cloves
- 1/2 tsp vanilla extract
- A pinch of sea salt
- Optional toppings: chopped walnuts, pumpkin seeds, coconut flakes, or a drizzle of extra maple syrup

Step-by-Step Directions:

1. Cook the Quinoa: I start by rinsing the quinoa thoroughly under cold water. Then, in a medium saucepan, combine the rinsed quinoa and almond milk. Bring the mixture to a gentle boil over medium heat.
2. Simmer and Season: Once the quinoa begins to boil, reduce the heat to low and cover the saucepan. Let it simmer for about 15 minutes, or until the quinoa is tender and has absorbed most of the liquid.
3. Add Pumpkin and Spices: After the quinoa is cooked, I stir in the pumpkin puree, maple syrup, cinnamon, nutmeg, ginger, cloves, vanilla extract, and a pinch of sea salt. Stir the mixture well to combine all the flavors.
4. Heat and Serve: Continue to cook the porridge for another 5 minutes, stirring occasionally, until it reaches your desired consistency. If the porridge becomes too thick, you can add a little more almond milk to thin it out.
5. Garnish and Enjoy: Pour the porridge into two bowls, and top with your choice of chopped walnuts, pumpkin seeds, coconut flakes, or an extra drizzle of maple syrup.

Nutritional Information (Per Serving):

- Calories: 230 | Protein: 6g | Fiber: 5g | Healthy Fats: 7g | Carbs: 35g

Tips:

1. Adjust the Sweetness: Feel free to adjust the amount of maple syrup to suit your taste.
2. Extra Creaminess: For a richer texture, you can use coconut milk instead of almond milk.
3. Texture Variety: Adding crunchy toppings like nuts or seeds enhances the texture and adds extra nutrients.

Serving Suggestions:

- I love serving this porridge warm, straight from the pot. It's perfect for a cozy breakfast, especially on cooler mornings. Pair it with a cup of herbal tea or a warm latte for a complete, satisfying meal.

Kale and Sweet Potato Breakfast Skillet

Gluten-Free, Soy-Free, Nut-Free

This Kale and Sweet Potato Breakfast Skillet is a hearty, nutritious dish that's perfect for starting your day with sustained energy. Packed with fiber, vitamins, and minerals, this gluten-free, soy-free, and nut-free meal is designed to support metabolic health and reduce inflammation, keeping you fueled and focused throughout the morning.

Prep time: 5 minutes | Cooking time: 20 minutes | Servings: 2

Ingredients:

- 1 large sweet potato, peeled and diced into small cubes
- 1 tbsp olive oil
- 1/2 red onion, finely chopped
- 1 red bell pepper, chopped
- 2 cups kale, chopped (stems removed)
- 2 garlic cloves, minced
- 1/2 tsp ground cumin
- 1/4 tsp smoked paprika
- 1/4 tsp ground turmeric
- Salt and pepper to taste
- 2 large eggs (optional, for additional protein)

Step-by-Step Directions:

1. Prepare the Sweet Potatoes: I start by heating a large skillet over medium heat. Add the olive oil to the skillet, and once it's hot, add the diced sweet potatoes. I like to cook them for about 10 minutes, stirring occasionally, until they become tender and slightly crispy on the edges.
2. Add the Vegetables: Once the sweet potatoes are nearly done, I add the chopped red onion and red bell pepper to the skillet. I sauté them for about 5 minutes until they soften and become fragrant.
3. Incorporate the Kale and Spices: Next, I add the chopped kale and minced garlic to the skillet. I sprinkle in the ground cumin, smoked paprika, ground turmeric, salt, and pepper. I continue to cook everything together for another 3-4 minutes until the kale wilts and the flavors meld together.
4. Cook the Eggs (Optional): If I'm adding eggs, I will create two small wells in the skillet and crack the eggs into each well. I cover the skillet with a lid and let the eggs cook for about 3-4 minutes until the whites are set but the yolks are still slightly runny. This step adds extra protein to the dish, making it even more satisfying.
5. Serve and Enjoy: Once everything is cooked, I divide the skillet between two plates. I like to serve it hot, straight from the skillet, and enjoy the blend of sweet, savory, and spicy flavors.

Nutritional Information (Per Serving):

- Calories: 280 | Protein: 5g | Fiber: 10g | Healthy Fats: 10g | Carbs: 35g

Tips:

1. Make it Vegan: Simply omit the eggs if you prefer a vegan version of this dish.
2. Add a Protein Boost: You can add some cooked black beans or crumbled tofu for additional protein.
3. Spice it Up: If you like more heat, try adding a pinch of cayenne pepper or red chili flakes.

Serving Suggestions:

- This skillet pairs well with a side of sliced avocado or a dollop of your favorite salsa. It's a perfect way to fuel your morning, whether you're heading out for a busy day or enjoying a relaxed breakfast at home.

Coconut Flour Waffles with Berry Compote

Gluten-Free, Dairy-Free, Soy-Free

These Coconut Flour Waffles topped with a fresh Berry Compote are the perfect start to your day. They're fluffy, delicious, and packed with nutrients that support metabolic health. This recipe is gluten-free, dairy-free, and soy-free, making it a wholesome breakfast option for everyone.

Prep time: 15 minutes | Cooking time: 20 minutes | Servings: Makes 4 waffles

Ingredients:

- For the Waffles:
- 1/2 cup coconut flour
- 1/4 cup tapioca flour
- 1/2 tsp baking soda
- 1/4 tsp sea salt
- 4 large eggs
- 1/2 cup almond milk (or any dairy-free milk)
- 2 tbsp coconut oil, melted
- 1 tbsp maple syrup (optional, for sweetness)
- 1 tsp vanilla extract
- For the Berry Compote:
- 1 cup mixed berries (strawberries, blueberries, raspberries)
- 1 tbsp water
- 1 tbsp lemon juice
- 1 tbsp maple syrup (optional)

Step-by-Step Directions:

1. Prepare the Waffle Batter: First, I whisk together the dry ingredients—coconut flour, tapioca flour, baking soda, and sea salt—in a large mixing bowl. In a separate bowl, I whisk the eggs, almond milk, melted coconut oil, maple syrup (if using), and vanilla extract until smooth. I then combine the wet and dry ingredients, mixing until I achieve a smooth batter. The batter will be thicker than traditional waffle batters, which is normal for coconut flour.
2. Cook the Waffles: I preheat my waffle iron and lightly grease it with some coconut oil. Once heated, I pour about 1/4 cup of the batter into the waffle iron, spreading it out evenly. I close the lid and cook for about 4-5 minutes, or until the waffles are golden and cooked through. I repeat this process with the remaining batter.
3. Make the Berry Compote: While the waffles are cooking, I prepare the berry compote. I combine the mixed berries, water, lemon juice, and maple syrup in a small saucepan over medium heat. I bring it to a simmer, stirring occasionally, until the berries break down and the sauce thickens slightly, about 5-7 minutes. I then remove it from heat and set it aside.
4. Serve: I like to serve the waffles warm, topped generously with the berry compote. The combination of the fluffy waffles and the sweet-tart berries makes for a delicious and satisfying breakfast.

Nutritional Information (Per Waffle with Compote):

- Calories: 220 | Protein: 7g | Fiber: 4g | Healthy Fats: 12g | Carbs: 18g

Tips:

1. For Extra Protein: Add a scoop of your favorite plant-based protein powder to the waffle batter.
2. Vegan Option: Replace the eggs with flax eggs (1 tbsp ground flaxseed + 3 tbsp water per egg) and increase the baking soda slightly to help with the rise.
3. Make Ahead: These waffles freeze well. I cool them completely and store them in an airtight container in the freezer. I reheat them in a toaster or oven when ready to eat.

Serving Suggestions:

These waffles pair well with a drizzle of almond butter or a sprinkle of unsweetened shredded coconut for added texture and flavor. Enjoy them with a side of fresh fruit or a cup of herbal tea for a balanced and energizing breakfast.

Egg White Veggie Scramble with Fresh Herbs

Gluten-Free, Soy-Free, Nut-Free

This Egg White Veggie Scramble is a light and protein-packed breakfast that's perfect for starting your day with sustained energy. Loaded with fresh vegetables and herbs, it's both nutritious and delicious. Plus, it's gluten-free, soy-free, and nut-free, making it a great option for various dietary needs.

Prep time: 10 minutes | Cooking time: 10 minutes | Servings: 2

Ingredients:

- 6 large egg whites
- 1/2 cup baby spinach, chopped
- 1/4 cup bell peppers, diced (any color)
- 1/4 cup cherry tomatoes, halved
- 1/4 cup red onion, finely chopped
- 1 tbsp fresh parsley, chopped
- 1 tbsp fresh chives, chopped
- 1 tbsp olive oil or avocado oil
- Sea salt and black pepper to taste
- 1/4 tsp turmeric (optional, for extra anti-inflammatory benefits)

Step-by-Step Directions:

1. Prepare the Vegetables: First, I'll gather all the veggies. I'll chop the baby spinach, dice the bell peppers, halve the cherry tomatoes, and finely chop the red onion. This helps ensure everything cooks evenly.
2. Cook the Vegetables: I'll heat a tablespoon of olive oil or avocado oil in a non-stick skillet over medium heat. Once the oil is hot, I'll add the chopped onions and bell peppers. I'll sauté them for about 2-3 minutes, until they begin to soften. Then, I'll add the cherry tomatoes and spinach, cooking for another minute or until the spinach wilts.
3. Scramble the Egg Whites: I'll pour the egg whites directly into the skillet with the vegetables. I'll gently stir everything together, making sure the eggs start to cook through. I'll season with sea salt, black pepper, and a pinch of turmeric if you're using it.
4. Add Fresh Herbs: Just before the eggs are fully set, I'll sprinkle in the fresh parsley and chives. I'll continue to stir the scramble until the eggs are fully cooked but still soft, about 1-2 minutes.
5. Serve: I'll transfer the scramble to plates and serve it hot. It's perfect on its own or paired with a slice of gluten-free toast or a side of avocado.

Nutritional Information (Per Serving):

- Calories: 120 | Protein: 12g | Fiber: 2g | Healthy Fats: 5g | Carbs: 6g

Tips:

1. Add More Veggies: Feel free to toss in other vegetables like zucchini or mushrooms if you want to mix it up.
2. Herb Variations: If you have other fresh herbs on hand, like basil or dill, you can use those for different flavor profiles.
3. Make It Heartier: Add a side of roasted sweet potatoes or a small portion of quinoa to make this meal even more filling.

Serving Suggestions:

- This scramble pairs wonderfully with a side of fresh fruit or a small green salad. It's also great with a dash of hot sauce or a sprinkle of nutritional yeast for added flavor.

LUNCH RECIPES
Lentil and Kale Salad with Lemon-Tahini Dressing
Gluten-Free, Dairy-Free, Soy-Free

This Lentil and Kale Salad with Lemon-Tahini Dressing is a satisfying and nutrient-packed lunch that I love to make. It's full of protein, fiber, and healthy fats that keep me energized throughout the day. The combination of earthy lentils and nutrient-dense kale, paired with a zesty lemon-tahini dressing, makes this salad not only delicious but also perfectly aligned with the Good Energy principles. It supports metabolic health, fights inflammation, and provides balanced nutrition, making it an ideal meal for midday.

Prep time: 15 minutes | Cooking time: 25 minutes | Servings: 2

Ingredients:

- For the Salad:
- 1 cup green or brown lentils, rinsed
- 4 cups kale, chopped and stems removed
- 1 small red onion, thinly sliced
- 1/2 cup cherry tomatoes, halved
- 1/4 cup sunflower seeds (for a bit of crunch)
- 1/4 cup fresh parsley, chopped
- For the Lemon-Tahini Dressing:
- 1/4 cup tahini
- 1/4 cup fresh lemon juice (about 1 lemon)
- 2 tablespoons extra-virgin olive oil
- 1 tablespoon maple syrup (optional, for sweetness)
- 1 clove garlic, minced
- 1/4 teaspoon sea salt
- 1/4 teaspoon black pepper
- 2-3 tablespoons water (to thin the dressing, if needed)

Step-by-Step Directions:

1. Cook the Lentils: I start by bringing a pot of water to a boil, then I add the rinsed lentils. I let them cook for about 20-25 minutes until they are tender but still firm to the bite. Once they're done, I drain them and set them aside to cool slightly.
2. Massage the Kale: While the lentils are cooking, I prepare the kale. I place the chopped kale in a large bowl, drizzle a bit of olive oil and a pinch of sea salt over it, and then massage the kale with my hands for about 2 minutes. This helps soften the kale and makes it easier to eat.
3. Prepare the Dressing: For the dressing, I whisk together the tahini, fresh lemon juice, olive oil, minced garlic, sea salt, and black pepper in a small bowl. If the dressing is too thick, I add 1 tablespoon of water at a time until I reach the desired consistency. The dressing should be smooth and pourable, with a bright, tangy flavor.
4. Assemble the Salad: Once the lentils have cooled slightly, I add them to the bowl with the kale. Then, I toss in the sliced red onion, cherry tomatoes, sunflower seeds, and chopped parsley. I pour the lemon-tahini dressing over the salad and toss everything together until it's well coated.
5. Serve and Enjoy: I divide the salad into two bowls and serve it immediately. The flavors come together beautifully, and it's a refreshing and nourishing meal that's perfect for lunch.

Nutritional Information (Per Serving):

- Calories: 420 | Protein: 18g | Fiber: 14g | Healthy Fats: 20g | Carbs: 40g

Tips:

1. Make It Ahead: This salad can be made ahead of time and stored in the fridge for up to 2 days. Just keep the dressing separate until you're ready to eat to prevent the salad from becoming soggy.
2. Add Protein: If you're looking for an extra protein boost, grilled chicken or tofu would make a great addition to this salad.

Grilled Chicken and Quinoa Stuffed Bell Peppers

Gluten-Free, Dairy-Free, Soy-Free

I love making these Grilled Chicken and Quinoa Stuffed Bell Peppers for lunch because they're packed with protein, fiber, and vibrant flavors that keep me full and energized for the rest of the day. The combination of lean grilled chicken, nutrient-dense quinoa, and colorful bell peppers creates a balanced and satisfying meal. This dish aligns perfectly with the Good Energy principles, focusing on metabolic health, anti-inflammatory ingredients, and balanced nutrition. It's a hearty and wholesome meal that's as delicious as it is nutritious.

Prep time: 15 minutes | Cooking time: 30 minutes | Servings: 4

Ingredients:

- For the Stuffed Bell Peppers:
- 4 large bell peppers, tops cut off and seeds removed
- 1 cup quinoa, rinsed
- 2 cups water or vegetable broth (for added flavor)
- 2 tablespoons extra-virgin olive oil
- 1 pound grilled chicken breast, diced
- 1 small red onion, finely chopped
- 2 cloves garlic, minced
- 1 cup cherry tomatoes, halved
- 1/2 cup fresh parsley, chopped
- 1/2 teaspoon smoked paprika
- 1/2 teaspoon ground cumin
- 1/4 teaspoon sea salt
- 1/4 teaspoon black pepper
- For the Garnish:
- 1 avocado, sliced
- Lemon wedges (optional, for serving)

Step-by-Step Directions:

1. Cook the Quinoa: I start by bringing 2 cups of water or vegetable broth to a boil in a medium saucepan. I add the rinsed quinoa, reduce the heat to low, cover, and let it simmer for about 15 minutes, or until the quinoa is tender and has absorbed all the liquid. Once it's done, I fluff it with a fork and set it aside.
2. Prepare the Chicken and Vegetables: While the quinoa is cooking, I heat 1 tablespoon of olive oil in a large skillet over medium heat. I add the diced red onion and cook for about 3-4 minutes until it becomes translucent. Then, I add the minced garlic, cherry tomatoes, smoked paprika, and ground cumin, cooking for another 2 minutes until everything is fragrant and well combined.
3. Combine the Filling: Next, I add the diced grilled chicken to the skillet, stirring to combine it with the vegetables. I then add the cooked quinoa to the mixture, along with the chopped parsley, sea salt, and black pepper. I stir everything together until it's well mixed and heated through.
4. Stuff the Bell Peppers: I preheat the oven to 375°F (190°C). I place the prepared bell peppers in a baking dish, then carefully spoon the chicken and quinoa mixture into each pepper until they're full. I drizzle the remaining olive oil over the stuffed peppers.
5. Bake the Stuffed Peppers: I cover the baking dish with foil and bake the peppers for 20 minutes. After 20 minutes, I remove the foil and bake for an additional 10 minutes, until the peppers are tender and slightly roasted on top.
6. Serve and Enjoy: I remove the stuffed peppers from the oven and let them cool slightly. I serve them with sliced avocado on top and a lemon wedge on the side for a fresh, zesty finish.

Nutritional Information (Per Serving): Calories: 450 | Protein: 28g | Fiber: 10g | Healthy Fats: 18g | Carbs: 42g

Tips:

1. Feel free to add other veggies like spinach or zucchini to the filling. They'll cook up nicely with the other ingredients.
2. Make It Ahead: You can prepare the stuffing ahead of time and refrigerate it. When you're ready to cook, just stuff the peppers and bake.

Roasted Beet and Arugula Salad with Walnuts and Goat Cheese

Gluten-Free, Soy-Free

This Roasted Beet and Arugula Salad is one of my go-to lunches when I want something light yet satisfying. The earthy sweetness of roasted beets pairs perfectly with the peppery arugula, crunchy walnuts, and creamy goat cheese. This salad is not only delicious but also packed with nutrients that support metabolic health and reduce inflammation. The ingredients are carefully chosen to align with the Good Energy principles, ensuring a balanced meal that keeps you energized throughout the day.

Prep time: 15 minutes | Cooking time: 40 minutes | Servings: 4

Ingredients:

- For the Salad:
- 4 medium beets, peeled and cut into wedges
- 6 cups fresh arugula, washed and dried
- 1/2 cup walnuts, lightly toasted
- 4 ounces goat cheese, crumbled
- 1 small red onion, thinly sliced
- 2 tablespoons extra-virgin olive oil (for roasting the beets)
- 1/4 teaspoon sea salt
- 1/4 teaspoon black pepper
- For the Dressing:
- 3 tablespoons extra-virgin olive oil
- 2 tablespoons balsamic vinegar
- 1 teaspoon Dijon mustard
- 1 teaspoon honey (optional, for sweetness)
- 1 clove garlic, minced
- 1/4 teaspoon sea salt
- 1/4 teaspoon black pepper

Step-by-Step Directions:

1. Roast the Beets: I start by preheating the oven to 400°F (200°C). I toss the beet wedges in 2 tablespoons of olive oil, sea salt, and black pepper, making sure they're evenly coated. I spread them out on a baking sheet lined with parchment paper and roast for about 35-40 minutes, turning halfway through, until they're tender and slightly caramelized. Once done, I let them cool slightly.
2. Prepare the Dressing: While the beets are roasting, I whisk together the extra-virgin olive oil, balsamic vinegar, Dijon mustard, honey (if using), minced garlic, sea salt, and black pepper in a small bowl until the dressing is well combined and smooth.
3. Assemble the Salad: In a large salad bowl, I combine the fresh arugula, toasted walnuts, and thinly sliced red onion. Once the roasted beets have cooled a bit, I add them to the salad. I then drizzle the dressing over the salad and toss everything gently to ensure the ingredients are well coated.
4. Add the Goat Cheese: Finally, I sprinkle the crumbled goat cheese over the top of the salad. The goat cheese adds a creamy texture that pairs beautifully with the earthy beets and tangy dressing.
5. Serve and Enjoy: I divide the salad into four portions and serve it immediately. It's a refreshing, nutrient-rich lunch that's perfect for a midday energy boost.

Nutritional Information (Per Serving):

- Calories: 320 | Protein: 9g | Fiber: 6g | Healthy Fats: 24g | Carbs: 20g

Tips:

1. Prepare Ahead: You can roast the beets and make the dressing ahead of time, storing them in the fridge until you're ready to assemble the salad. This makes it a quick and easy lunch option during the week.
2. Add Protein: If you'd like to add more protein, grilled chicken or chickpeas would make a great addition to this salad.

Chickpea and Avocado Lettuce Wraps

Gluten-Free, Dairy-Free, Soy-Free, Nut-Free

These Chickpea and Avocado Lettuce Wraps are one of my favorite lunch options when I'm craving something light yet satisfying. They're packed with plant-based protein, healthy fats, and plenty of fiber to keep me full and energized throughout the afternoon. The combination of creamy avocado and chickpeas with crisp lettuce makes for a refreshing and delicious meal. This recipe perfectly aligns with the Good Energy principles, focusing on balanced nutrition, anti-inflammatory ingredients, and metabolic health.

Prep time: 10 minutes | Cooking time: None | Servings: 4 (2 wraps per serving)

Ingredients:

- 1 can (15 ounces) chickpeas, drained and rinsed
- 1 large ripe avocado, peeled and pitted
- 1/4 cup red onion, finely chopped
- 1/4 cup fresh cilantro, chopped
- Juice of 1 lime
- 1/2 teaspoon ground cumin
- 1/4 teaspoon smoked paprika
- 1/4 teaspoon sea salt
- 1/4 teaspoon black pepper
- 8 large lettuce leaves (such as romaine or butter lettuce)
- 1/2 cup cherry tomatoes, halved
- 1 small cucumber, diced

Step-by-Step Directions:

1. Mash the Chickpeas and Avocado: I start by placing the drained chickpeas in a large mixing bowl. Using a fork or potato masher, I gently mash the chickpeas until they're slightly broken down but still chunky. Then, I add the avocado and continue mashing until the mixture is creamy but still has some texture.
2. Mix in the Veggies and Spices: Next, I stir in the finely chopped red onion, fresh cilantro, lime juice, ground cumin, smoked paprika, sea salt, and black pepper. I mix everything together until it's well combined. The lime juice adds a refreshing tang, while the spices provide a warm, earthy flavor that complements the creaminess of the avocado.
3. Assemble the Lettuce Wraps: I lay out the large lettuce leaves on a clean surface. I spoon the chickpea and avocado mixture evenly into the center of each leaf. Then, I top the mixture with halved cherry tomatoes and diced cucumber for extra crunch and freshness.
4. Serve and Enjoy: I carefully fold the lettuce leaves around the filling to create wraps. These wraps are best enjoyed immediately while the lettuce is crisp and the flavors are fresh.

Nutritional Information (Per Serving):

- Calories: 250 | Protein: 7g | Fiber: 10g | Healthy Fats: 14g | Carbs: 26g

Tips:

1. Make It Ahead: You can prepare the chickpea and avocado mixture ahead of time and store it in the fridge. Just assemble the wraps right before serving to keep the lettuce crisp.
2. Add a Kick: If you like a bit of heat, add a pinch of red pepper flakes or a drizzle of hot sauce to the chickpea mixture.

Serving Suggestions:

- These lettuce wraps are perfect on their own, but if you're looking for a more filling meal, you can pair them with a side of quinoa or a light vegetable soup. They're also great with a refreshing iced tea or a citrus-infused water.

Shrimp and Cucumber Salad with Citrus Vinaigrette

Gluten-Free, Dairy-Free, Soy-Free, Nut-Free

This Shrimp and Cucumber Salad with Citrus Vinaigrette is one of my favorite lunches because it's light, refreshing, and packed with flavors that wake up your taste buds. The shrimp provides a lean source of protein, while the cucumber adds a crisp, hydrating crunch. The citrus vinaigrette ties everything together with a bright, zesty kick. This salad is not only delicious but also perfectly aligns with the Good Energy principles, supporting metabolic health, reducing inflammation, and offering balanced nutrition.

Prep time: 15 minutes | Cooking time: 10 minutes | Servings: 4

Ingredients:

- For the Salad:
- 1 pound large shrimp, peeled and deveined
- 4 cups cucumber, thinly sliced (about 2 large cucumbers)
- 1 small red onion, thinly sliced
- 1 avocado, diced
- 1/4 cup fresh cilantro, chopped
- 4 cups mixed greens (such as arugula or spinach)

- For the Citrus Vinaigrette:
- 1/4 cup fresh orange juice (about 1 orange)
- 2 tablespoons fresh lime juice (about 1 lime)
- 2 tablespoons extra-virgin olive oil
- 1 teaspoon Dijon mustard
- 1 teaspoon honey (optional, for sweetness)
- 1 clove garlic, minced
- 1/4 teaspoon sea salt
- 1/4 teaspoon black pepper

Step-by-Step Directions:

1. Cook the Shrimp: I start by heating a large skillet over medium heat with a tablespoon of olive oil. Once the oil is hot, I add the shrimp, seasoning them with a pinch of sea salt and black pepper. I cook the shrimp for about 2-3 minutes on each side, until they're pink and opaque. Once cooked, I remove them from the heat and let them cool slightly.
2. Prepare the Salad Base: While the shrimp is cooling, I arrange the mixed greens on a large serving platter or in individual bowls. Then, I top the greens with the sliced cucumber, red onion, diced avocado, and chopped cilantro.
3. Make the Citrus Vinaigrette: In a small bowl, I whisk together the fresh orange juice, lime juice, extra-virgin olive oil, Dijon mustard, honey (if using), minced garlic, sea salt, and black pepper. The vinaigrette should be smooth and well-emulsified, with a bright citrus flavor that complements the salad ingredients perfectly.
4. Assemble the Salad: Once the shrimp has cooled slightly, I arrange them on top of the salad. Then, I drizzle the citrus vinaigrette over the entire salad, making sure everything is evenly coated with the tangy dressing.
5. Serve and Enjoy: I serve the salad immediately, ensuring each serving gets plenty of shrimp, crisp cucumber, and creamy avocado. The combination of textures and flavors makes this salad both refreshing and satisfying.

Nutritional Information (Per Serving):

- Calories: 320 | Protein: 24g | Fiber: 6g | Healthy Fats: 18g | Carbs: 18g

Tips:

1. Chill the Salad: For an even more refreshing dish, you can chill the cucumber and mixed greens in the fridge before assembling the salad.
2. Make It Ahead: The shrimp can be cooked and the vinaigrette prepared in advance. Just store them in the fridge and assemble the salad right before serving to keep everything fresh and crisp.

Grilled Chicken and Avocado Salad with Lemon-Basil Vinaigrette

Gluten-Free, Dairy-Free, Soy-Free, Nut-Free

This is my go-to lunch when I'm craving something light yet satisfying. The grilled chicken provides lean protein, while the avocado offers healthy fats that keep me full and energized. The lemon-basil vinaigrette adds a bright, fresh flavor that ties everything together beautifully. This salad aligns perfectly with the Good Energy principles, supporting metabolic health and providing balanced nutrition with anti-inflammatory ingredients.

Prep time: 15 minutes | Cooking time: 15 minutes | Servings: 4

Ingredients:

- For the Salad:
- 1 pound chicken breast, boneless and skinless
- 6 cups mixed greens (such as arugula, spinach, and romaine)
- 2 large avocados, sliced
- 1 cucumber, sliced
- 1 cup cherry tomatoes, halved
- 1/4 cup red onion, thinly sliced
- 1 tablespoon extra-virgin olive oil (for grilling the chicken)
- 1/4 teaspoon sea salt
- 1/4 teaspoon black pepper
- For the Lemon-Basil Vinaigrette:
- 1/4 cup fresh lemon juice (about 1 large lemon)
- 1/4 cup extra-virgin olive oil
- 1 tablespoon fresh basil, finely chopped
- 1 teaspoon Dijon mustard
- 1 clove garlic, minced
- 1 teaspoon honey (optional, for sweetness)
- 1/4 teaspoon sea salt
- 1/4 teaspoon black pepper

Step-by-Step Directions:

1. Grill the Chicken: I start by seasoning the chicken breasts with sea salt and black pepper on both sides. Then, I heat a grill pan or outdoor grill over medium heat and brush it lightly with olive oil. I place the chicken on the grill and cook for about 6-7 minutes on each side, or until the chicken is cooked through and has nice grill marks. Once done, I remove the chicken from the grill and let it rest for a few minutes before slicing it into strips.
2. Prepare the Salad Base: While the chicken is grilling, I arrange the mixed greens on a large serving platter or in individual bowls. I then add the sliced avocado, cucumber, cherry tomatoes, and red onion on top of the greens. The combination of these fresh vegetables adds a variety of textures and flavors to the salad.
3. Make the Lemon-Basil Vinaigrette: In a small bowl, I whisk together the fresh lemon juice, extra-virgin olive oil, chopped basil, Dijon mustard, minced garlic, sea salt, and black pepper. If I want a touch of sweetness, I add a teaspoon of honey. The vinaigrette should be smooth and well-emulsified, with a bright, zesty flavor.
4. Assemble the Salad: Once the chicken is ready and sliced, I arrange it on top of the salad. I then drizzle the lemon-basil vinaigrette over the entire salad, making sure everything is well coated. The vinaigrette brings a refreshing citrusy flavor that pairs perfectly with the grilled chicken and creamy avocado.
5. Serve and Enjoy: I serve the salad immediately, ensuring each serving includes a generous amount of chicken, avocado, and fresh vegetables. This salad is filling, flavorful, and perfect for a nourishing lunch.

Nutritional Information (Per Serving):

Calories: 400 | Protein: 28g | Fiber: 9g | Healthy Fats: 28g | Carbs: 16g

Tips:

1. Marinate the Chicken: For extra flavor, you can marinate the chicken in a little bit of the lemon-basil vinaigrette for 30 minutes before grilling.

Mediterranean Chickpea Salad with Cucumber and Feta

Gluten-Free, Soy-Free

This Mediterranean Chickpea Salad with Cucumber and Feta is one of my favorite lunch options because it's refreshing, full of flavor, and packed with nutrients that keep me energized throughout the day. The chickpeas provide plant-based protein and fiber, while the cucumber adds a hydrating crunch. Feta cheese adds a creamy, tangy element that brings all the flavors together. This salad aligns perfectly with the Good Energy principles, focusing on metabolic health, anti-inflammatory ingredients, and balanced nutrition.

Prep time: 15 minutes | Cooking time: None | Servings: 4

Ingredients:

- For the Salad:
- 2 cups canned chickpeas, drained and rinsed
- 2 cups cucumber, diced (about 1 large cucumber)
- 1 cup cherry tomatoes, halved
- 1/2 cup red onion, finely chopped
- 1/2 cup Kalamata olives, pitted and sliced
- 1/2 cup feta cheese, crumbled
- 1/4 cup fresh parsley, chopped

- For the Dressing:
- 1/4 cup extra-virgin olive oil
- 2 tablespoons fresh lemon juice (about 1 lemon)
- 1 tablespoon red wine vinegar
- 1 clove garlic, minced
- 1 teaspoon dried oregano
- 1/4 teaspoon sea salt
- 1/4 teaspoon black pepper

Step-by-Step Directions:

1. Prepare the Salad Base: I start by combining the chickpeas, diced cucumber, cherry tomatoes, red onion, Kalamata olives, and chopped parsley in a large mixing bowl. The combination of these fresh ingredients provides a variety of textures and flavors that make this salad both satisfying and nutritious.
2. Make the Dressing: In a small bowl, I whisk together the extra-virgin olive oil, fresh lemon juice, red wine vinegar, minced garlic, dried oregano, sea salt, and black pepper. The dressing should be smooth and well-emulsified, with a bright, tangy flavor that complements the salad perfectly.
3. Combine the Salad and Dressing: I pour the dressing over the salad and toss everything together until the ingredients are well coated. This step ensures that every bite is packed with flavor and that the salad remains light and refreshing.
4. Add the Feta Cheese: Finally, I gently fold in the crumbled feta cheese. The feta adds a creamy texture and a deliciously tangy taste that balances the freshness of the vegetables and the heartiness of the chickpeas.
5. Serve and Enjoy: I divide the salad into four portions and serve it immediately. It's a perfect lunch option that's both filling and energizing, keeping you satisfied throughout the day.

Nutritional Information (Per Serving):

- Calories: 320 | Protein: 10g | Fiber: 8g | Healthy Fats: 20g | Carbs: 28g

Tips:

1. Make It Ahead: This salad can be made ahead of time and stored in the fridge for up to 2 days. Just keep the dressing separate until you're ready to eat to maintain the salad's crispness.
2. Add Protein: If you're looking for an extra protein boost, grilled chicken or tuna would be great additions to this salad.

Spicy Lentil Soup with Carrots and Kale

Gluten-Free, Dairy-Free, Soy-Free, Nut-Free

This Spicy Lentil Soup with Carrots and Kale is a warming, nourishing lunch that I often turn to when I need something hearty yet healthy. The lentils provide a great source of plant-based protein and fiber, while the carrots and kale add a wealth of vitamins and minerals. The spice in this soup not only adds flavor but also supports metabolism and inflammation reduction. This recipe aligns perfectly with the Good Energy principles, focusing on balanced nutrition and ingredients that promote metabolic health.

Prep time: 15 minutes | Cooking time: 35 minutes | Servings: 4

Ingredients:

- 1 cup dried lentils, rinsed
- 1 tablespoon extra-virgin olive oil
- 1 large onion, finely chopped
- 2 cloves garlic, minced
- 3 large carrots, sliced
- 1 teaspoon ground cumin
- 1 teaspoon ground turmeric
- 1/2 teaspoon smoked paprika

- 1/4 teaspoon cayenne pepper (adjust to taste)
- 6 cups vegetable broth (or water)
- 4 cups kale, chopped (stems removed)
- 1 bay leaf
- Juice of 1 lemon
- 1/2 teaspoon sea salt
- 1/4 teaspoon black pepper
- Fresh parsley, chopped, for garnish (optional)

Step-by-Step Directions:

1. Sauté the Vegetables: I start by heating the olive oil in a large pot over medium heat. Once the oil is hot, I add the chopped onion and sauté for about 5 minutes until it becomes translucent. Then, I add the minced garlic and sliced carrots, cooking for another 3 minutes until the carrots begin to soften.
2. Add the Spices: Next, I stir in the ground cumin, turmeric, smoked paprika, and cayenne pepper. I let the spices cook for about 1 minute to release their flavors, ensuring the soup has a deep, rich taste.
3. Cook the Lentils: I add the rinsed lentils to the pot, stirring them to coat with the spices. Then, I pour in the vegetable broth and add the bay leaf. I bring the soup to a boil, then reduce the heat to low, covering the pot and letting the soup simmer for about 25 minutes, or until the lentils are tender.
4. Add the Kale: Once the lentils are cooked, I stir in the chopped kale and let it cook for another 5 minutes until it's wilted and tender. This adds a boost of nutrients and a lovely green color to the soup.
5. Finish and Serve: I remove the bay leaf and stir in the lemon juice, sea salt, and black pepper. I taste the soup and adjust the seasoning if needed. I like to serve the soup hot, garnished with fresh parsley for a burst of freshness.

Nutritional Information (Per Serving):

- Calories: 280 | Protein: 15g | Fiber: 12g | Healthy Fats: 6g | Carbs: 42g

Tips:

1. Adjust the Spice: If you prefer a milder soup, you can reduce the amount of cayenne pepper or omit it altogether.
2. Make It Ahead: This soup keeps well in the refrigerator for up to 3 days and the flavors only get better with time. It can also be frozen for up to 2 months.

Grilled Veggie and Quinoa Stuffed Zucchini Boats

Gluten-Free, Dairy-Free, Soy-Free, Nut-Free

These Grilled Veggie and Quinoa Stuffed Zucchini Boats are a delicious and nutritious lunch option that I love to make when I'm in the mood for something light yet satisfying. The zucchini boats are filled with a flavorful mixture of grilled vegetables and quinoa, providing a great balance of protein, fiber, and healthy fats. This dish is packed with vitamins and minerals, supports metabolic health, and reduces inflammation, making it a perfect example of a Good Energy recipe.

Prep time: 20 minutes | Cooking time: 25 minutes | Servings: 4

Ingredients:

- For the Zucchini Boats:
- 4 large zucchinis, halved lengthwise
- 1 cup quinoa, rinsed
- 2 cups vegetable broth (or water)
- 1 red bell pepper, diced
- 1 yellow bell pepper, diced
- 1 small red onion, finely chopped
- 1 cup cherry tomatoes, halved
- 1 tablespoon extra-virgin olive oil
- 1 teaspoon smoked paprika
- 1 teaspoon ground cumin
- 1/2 teaspoon sea salt
- 1/4 teaspoon black pepper
- 1/4 cup fresh parsley, chopped (for garnish)

Step-by-Step Directions:

1. Cook the Quinoa: I begin by bringing the vegetable broth to a boil in a medium saucepan. I add the rinsed quinoa, reduce the heat to low, cover the pot, and let it simmer for about 15 minutes, or until the quinoa is tender and has absorbed all the liquid. Once cooked, I fluff the quinoa with a fork and set it aside.
2. Prepare the Zucchini Boats: While the quinoa is cooking, I preheat my grill (or grill pan) to medium heat. I scoop out the flesh from the zucchini halves using a spoon, leaving about 1/4-inch of the flesh intact to form a boat. I brush the zucchini boats with olive oil and season them with sea salt and black pepper.
3. Grill the Zucchini and Veggies: I place the zucchini boats on the grill, cut side down, and grill for about 5-7 minutes until they have nice grill marks and are slightly tender. At the same time, I grill the diced bell peppers, red onion, and cherry tomatoes until they are slightly charred and tender, about 5 minutes. Once done, I remove everything from the grill and set it aside.
4. Mix the Filling: In a large mixing bowl, I combine the cooked quinoa with the grilled vegetables. I add the smoked paprika, ground cumin, sea salt, and black pepper, stirring everything together until well combined.
5. Stuff the Zucchini Boats: I carefully spoon the quinoa and veggie mixture into each zucchini boat, packing it in well. I place the stuffed zucchini boats on a baking sheet and bake them in a preheated oven at 375°F (190°C) for about 10 minutes to heat through.
6. Serve and Enjoy: I garnish the stuffed zucchini boats with fresh parsley before serving. These boats are best enjoyed warm and are perfect for a satisfying, nutrient-rich lunch.

Nutritional Information (Per Serving):

- Calories: 280 | Protein: 8g | Fiber: 6g | Healthy Fats: 10g | Carbs: 38g

Tips:

1. Add Protein: If you'd like to add more protein, grilled chicken or chickpeas would make a great addition to the filling.
2. Make It Ahead: You can prepare the quinoa and veggie mixture ahead of time and store it in the fridge. Just stuff the zucchini boats and bake them when you're ready to serve.

Tuna Salad Lettuce Wraps with Avocado and Tomato

Gluten-Free, Dairy-Free, Soy-Free, Nut-Free

These Tuna Salad Lettuce Wraps with Avocado and Tomato are a quick, easy, and nutritious lunch option that I love to prepare. The combination of protein-rich tuna, creamy avocado, and fresh tomatoes wrapped in crisp lettuce makes for a satisfying meal that supports metabolic health and keeps you feeling full and energized. This recipe is perfectly aligned with the Good Energy principles, focusing on anti-inflammatory ingredients and balanced nutrition to promote overall well-being.

Prep time: 10 minutes | Cooking time: None | Servings: 4 (2 wraps per serving)

Ingredients:

- For the Tuna Salad:
- 2 cans (5 ounces each) tuna in water, drained
- 1 large avocado, peeled, pitted, and diced
- 1/4 cup red onion, finely chopped
- 1 tablespoon fresh lemon juice
- 1 tablespoon extra-virgin olive oil
- 1 teaspoon Dijon mustard
- 1/4 teaspoon sea salt
- 1/4 teaspoon black pepper
- 1 tablespoon fresh parsley, chopped (optional)
- For the Wraps:
- 8 large lettuce leaves (such as romaine, butter lettuce, or iceberg)
- 1 cup cherry tomatoes, halved
- 1/2 cucumber, sliced

Step-by-Step Directions:

1. Prepare the Tuna Salad: I start by flaking the drained tuna into a large mixing bowl. I then add the diced avocado, finely chopped red onion, fresh lemon juice, extra-virgin olive oil, Dijon mustard, sea salt, and black pepper. I gently mix everything together until the ingredients are well combined, and the tuna is coated in the creamy avocado mixture. If I'm using parsley, I add it at this stage for a bit of freshness.
2. Assemble the Lettuce Wraps: I lay out the large lettuce leaves on a clean surface. I spoon the tuna salad mixture evenly into the center of each leaf. Then, I top the tuna salad with halved cherry tomatoes and cucumber slices. These fresh toppings add a nice crunch and vibrant flavor to the wraps.
3. Fold and Serve: I carefully fold the lettuce leaves around the filling to create wraps. These wraps are best enjoyed immediately while the lettuce is crisp, and the flavors are fresh.

Nutritional Information (Per Serving):

- Calories: 260 | Protein: 20g | Fiber: 7g | Healthy Fats: 18g | Carbs: 10g

Tips:

1. Make It Ahead: You can prepare the tuna salad ahead of time and store it in the fridge. Just assemble the wraps right before serving to keep the lettuce crisp.
2. Add a Kick: If you like a bit of spice, add a pinch of red pepper flakes or a dash of hot sauce to the tuna salad mixture.

Serving Suggestions:

- These Tuna Salad Lettuce Wraps are perfect on their own, but I sometimes like to serve them with a side of sweet potato fries or a light quinoa salad for a more filling lunch. They're also great paired with a refreshing glass of iced herbal tea or infused water.

Eggplant and Bell Pepper Caponata with Fresh Herbs

Gluten-Free, Dairy-Free, Soy-Free, Nut-Free

This Eggplant and Bell Pepper Caponata is a delicious and versatile lunch option that's bursting with flavors. The combination of roasted eggplant, bell peppers, and a medley of fresh herbs creates a dish that's rich in antioxidants, fiber, and anti-inflammatory compounds. It's a great way to enjoy a variety of vegetables in one meal while supporting metabolic health and balanced nutrition. This recipe aligns perfectly with the Good Energy principles, making it a go-to for a healthy, satisfying lunch.

Prep time: 15 minutes | Cooking time: 30 minutes | Servings: 4

Ingredients:

- 1 large eggplant, diced into 1-inch cubes
- 2 bell peppers (red, yellow, or orange), diced into 1-inch pieces
- 1 small red onion, finely chopped
- 2 cloves garlic, minced
- 2 tablespoons extra-virgin olive oil
- 1 tablespoon capers, drained and rinsed
- 1/4 cup pitted Kalamata olives, chopped
- 1/4 cup tomato paste
- 1/4 cup balsamic vinegar
- 1 tablespoon fresh basil, chopped
- 1 tablespoon fresh parsley, chopped
- 1 teaspoon dried oregano
- 1/2 teaspoon sea salt
- 1/4 teaspoon black pepper
- 1/4 teaspoon crushed red pepper flakes (optional, for a bit of heat)

Step-by-Step Directions:

1. Prepare the Vegetables: I start by preheating the oven to 400°F (200°C). I toss the diced eggplant and bell peppers with 1 tablespoon of extra-virgin olive oil, sea salt, and black pepper. I spread the vegetables out on a baking sheet lined with parchment paper and roast them in the preheated oven for about 20-25 minutes, or until they are tender and slightly caramelized.
2. Sauté the Onions and Garlic: While the vegetables are roasting, I heat the remaining 1 tablespoon of olive oil in a large skillet over medium heat. I add the chopped red onion and sauté for about 5 minutes until it becomes soft and translucent. Then, I add the minced garlic and cook for another minute until fragrant.
3. Combine the Ingredients: Once the vegetables are done roasting, I add them to the skillet with the sautéed onions and garlic. I stir in the capers, chopped olives, tomato paste, and balsamic vinegar. I let the mixture simmer for about 10 minutes, stirring occasionally, to allow the flavors to meld together.
4. Add the Fresh Herbs: Just before serving, I stir in the fresh basil, parsley, and dried oregano. If you like a bit of heat, you can add the crushed red pepper flakes at this stage as well. The fresh herbs add a burst of flavor and brightness to the dish.
5. Serve and Enjoy: I serve the caponata warm, either on its own or with a side of quinoa or gluten-free bread. The combination of textures and flavors makes this a hearty and satisfying lunch.

Nutritional Information (Per Serving):

- Calories: 220 | Protein: 4g | Fiber: 8g | Healthy Fats: 14g | Carbs: 22g

Tips:

1. Make It Ahead: This caponata can be made ahead of time and stored in the fridge for up to 3 days. The flavors only get better as they sit, making it an ideal meal prep option.
2. Serve It Cold: This dish is also delicious served cold as a topping for salads or as a dip for vegetables.

Asian-Inspired Salmon Salad with Sesame-Ginger Dressing

Gluten-Free, Dairy-Free, Soy-Free, Nut-Free

This is a flavorful, nutrient-packed lunch that I love to prepare when I need something light yet satisfying. The salmon provides a rich source of omega-3 fatty acids, which are essential for metabolic health and reducing inflammation. Paired with fresh, crisp vegetables and a tangy sesame-ginger dressing, this salad is both delicious and perfectly aligned with the Good Energy principles.

Prep time: 15 minutes | Cooking time: 10 minutes | Servings: 4

Ingredients:

- For the Salad:
- 4 salmon fillets (about 4-6 ounces each)
- 6 cups mixed greens (such as arugula, spinach, and romaine)
- 1 cucumber, thinly sliced
- 1 red bell pepper, thinly sliced
- 2 carrots, julienned or grated
- 2 green onions, thinly sliced
- 1 tablespoon extra-virgin olive oil (for cooking the salmon)
- 1/4 teaspoon sea salt
- 1/4 teaspoon black pepper
- For the Sesame-Ginger Dressing:
- 1/4 cup extra-virgin olive oil
- 2 tablespoons sesame oil (optional if you are not strictly nut-free)
- 2 tablespoons fresh lime juice (about 1 lime)
- 1 tablespoon coconut aminos (or tamari for soy-free option)
- 1 tablespoon rice vinegar
- 1 tablespoon fresh ginger, grated
- 1 clove garlic, minced
- 1 teaspoon honey (optional, for sweetness)
- 1/4 teaspoon sea salt
- 1/4 teaspoon black pepper

Step-by-Step Directions:

1. Cook the Salmon: I start by heating the olive oil in a large skillet over medium heat. I season the salmon fillets with sea salt and black pepper, then place them skin-side down in the skillet. I cook the salmon for about 4-5 minutes on each side, or until it's cooked through and flakes easily with a fork. Once done, I remove the salmon from the heat and let it cool slightly.
2. Prepare the Salad Base: While the salmon is cooking, I arrange the mixed greens on a large serving platter or in individual bowls. I then add the sliced cucumber, red bell pepper, carrots, and green onions on top of the greens. The variety of fresh vegetables adds a nice crunch and vibrant color to the salad.
3. Make the Sesame-Ginger Dressing: In a small bowl, I whisk together the extra-virgin olive oil, sesame oil (if using), fresh lime juice, coconut aminos, rice vinegar, grated ginger, minced garlic, honey (if using), sea salt, and black pepper. The dressing should be smooth, with a balanced tangy and slightly sweet flavor.
4. Assemble the Salad: I place the cooked salmon fillets on top of the salad and drizzle the sesame-ginger dressing over the entire dish. I like to flake the salmon into bite-sized pieces before serving, making it easier to enjoy with the salad.
5. Serve and Enjoy: I serve the salad immediately, making sure each serving gets a generous amount of salmon and a drizzle of the delicious dressing. The combination of flavors and textures makes this salad both refreshing and satisfying.

Nutritional Information (Per Serving):

- Calories: 420 | Protein: 28g | Fiber: 6g | Healthy Fats: 30g | Carbs: 12g

Tips:

1. Customize It: Feel free to add other vegetables like snap peas or radishes for extra crunch and flavor.
2. Make It Ahead: The sesame-ginger dressing can be made ahead of time and stored in the fridge for up to a week. Just shake or whisk it again before using.

Grilled Salmon with Quinoa and Avocado Salsa

Gluten-Free, Dairy-Free, *Soy*-Free

This Grilled Salmon with Quinoa and Avocado Salsa is a powerhouse lunch that supports your metabolic health and provides sustained energy throughout the day. Combining protein-rich salmon with fiber-packed quinoa and healthy fats from avocado, this dish is both satisfying and nutritious. It's gluten-free, dairy-free, and soy-free, making it suitable for a wide range of dietary needs.

Prep time: 15 minutes | Cooking time: 20 minutes | Servings: 2

Ingredients:

- For the Salmon:
- 2 salmon fillets (about 4-6 oz each)
- 1 tbsp olive oil
- Juice of 1/2 lemon
- 1 tsp garlic powder
- 1 tsp smoked paprika
- Sea salt and black pepper to taste
- For the Quinoa:
- 1/2 cup quinoa, rinsed
- 1 cup water or low-sodium vegetable broth
- Pinch of sea salt
- For the Avocado Salsa:
- 1 ripe avocado, diced
- 1/2 small red onion, finely chopped
- 1 small tomato, diced
- 1 tbsp fresh cilantro, chopped
- Juice of 1 lime
- Sea salt and black pepper to taste

Step-by-Step Directions:

1. Prepare the Quinoa: I'll start by rinsing the quinoa under cold water to remove any bitterness. I'll then combine the quinoa and water (or broth) in a small pot, add a pinch of salt, and bring it to a boil over medium heat. Once boiling, I'll reduce the heat to low, cover the pot, and let it simmer for about 15 minutes until the quinoa is tender and the water is absorbed. I'll fluff it with a fork and set it aside.
2. Season the Salmon: While the quinoa is cooking, I'll prepare the salmon. I'll rub the salmon fillets with olive oil, then sprinkle them with garlic powder, smoked paprika, salt, and pepper. I'll also squeeze a bit of lemon juice over the fillets for a fresh, zesty flavor.
3. Grill the Salmon: I'll preheat my grill or a grill pan over medium-high heat. Once it's hot, I'll place the salmon fillets skin-side down on the grill. I'll cook them for about 4-5 minutes per side, depending on thickness, until the fish is opaque and flakes easily with a fork.
4. Prepare the Avocado Salsa: While the salmon is grilling, I'll make the avocado salsa. I'll combine the diced avocado, red onion, tomato, and cilantro in a bowl. I'll then add lime juice, and a pinch of salt and pepper, and gently toss everything together.
5. Assemble the Dish: To serve, I'll place a generous spoonful of quinoa on each plate, top it with a grilled salmon fillet, and finish with a large spoonful of avocado salsa. The combination of textures and flavors is both refreshing and hearty.

Nutritional Information (Per Serving):

- Calories: 450 | Protein: 35g | Fiber: 8g | Healthy Fats: 25g | Carbs: 25g

Tips:

1. Customize the Salsa: Feel free to add a little diced jalapeño if you like a bit of heat in your salsa.
2. If quinoa isn't your preference, you can substitute it with brown rice or another gluten-free grain.
3. Cooking Indoors: If grilling isn't an option, you can pan-sear the salmon in a hot skillet for similar results.

Zucchini Ribbon Salad with Lemon-Tahini Dressing

Gluten-Free, Dairy-Free, Soy-Free, Nut-Free

This Zucchini Ribbon Salad with Lemon-Tahini Dressing is a light, refreshing, and nutrient-packed lunch that aligns with the Good Energy principles. It's perfect for continuing your day with a meal that supports metabolic health and provides sustained energy. The combination of fresh zucchini, vibrant herbs, and a creamy lemon-tahini dressing offers a delicious balance of flavors and textures. Plus, it's gluten-free, dairy-free, soy-free, and nut-free.

Prep time: 15 minutes | Servings: 2

Ingredients:

- For the Salad:
- 2 medium zucchinis, ends trimmed
- 1 small cucumber, ends trimmed
- 1/4 cup fresh parsley, chopped
- 1/4 cup fresh mint leaves, chopped
- 1/2 small red onion, thinly sliced
- 1 tbsp sesame seeds (optional)
- For the Lemon-Tahini Dressing:

- 2 tbsp tahini
- Juice of 1 lemon
- 1 tbsp extra-virgin olive oil
- 1 clove garlic, minced
- 1 tsp maple syrup or honey (optional)
- Sea salt and black pepper to taste
- 2-3 tbsp water, to thin the dressing to desired consistency

Step-by-Step Directions:

1. Prepare the Zucchini Ribbons: I'll start by using a vegetable peeler or a mandoline to slice the zucchinis and cucumber into thin ribbons. I'll set them aside in a large mixing bowl. The ribbons should be thin enough to easily roll or fold, creating a beautiful texture for the salad.
2. Chop the Herbs: Next, I'll chop the parsley and mint leaves, then add them to the bowl with the zucchini and cucumber ribbons. The fresh herbs add a burst of flavor and a vibrant green color to the salad.
3. Make the Lemon-Tahini Dressing: For the dressing, I'll whisk together the tahini, lemon juice, olive oil, minced garlic, and a touch of maple syrup or honey if I prefer a slightly sweeter dressing. I'll season it with salt and pepper, and gradually add water, one tablespoon at a time, until the dressing reaches a smooth, pourable consistency.
4. Assemble the Salad: I'll pour the lemon-tahini dressing over the zucchini ribbons and herbs. Using clean hands or salad tongs, I'll gently toss the salad until the ribbons are evenly coated with the dressing. I'll add the thinly sliced red onion and sesame seeds for extra crunch and flavor.
5. Serve: I'll divide the salad between two plates, ensuring each serving gets a good mix of zucchini ribbons, herbs, and red onion. The salad is now ready to enjoy as a light, refreshing breakfast that's full of good energy.

Nutritional Information (Per Serving):

- Calories: 180 | Protein: 4g | Fiber: 4g | Healthy Fats: 10g | Carbs: 14g

Tips:

1. Add Protein: If you want to make this salad more filling, you can add some grilled chicken or a poached egg on top for added protein.
2. Make Ahead: You can prepare the zucchini ribbons and the dressing in advance, but wait to dress the salad until just before serving to keep the zucchini fresh and crisp.
3. Extra Flavor: For added zest, consider sprinkling some lemon zest on top of the salad just before serving.

Stuffed Bell Peppers with Lentils and Spinach

Gluten-Free, Dairy-*Free*, Soy-Free

These Stuffed Bell Peppers with Lentils and Spinach are a hearty, nutritious, and energizing lunch option that aligns with the principles of Good Energy. Packed with protein, fiber, and leafy greens, this dish is perfect for kickstarting your day with balanced nutrition that supports metabolic health.

Prep time: 20 minutes | Cooking time: 30 minutes | Servings: 4

Ingredients:

- For the Stuffed Bell Peppers:
- 4 large bell peppers (any color), tops cut off and seeds removed
- 1 cup cooked lentils (green or brown)
- 1 cup fresh spinach, chopped
- 1 small onion, finely chopped
- 2 cloves garlic, minced
- 1 tbsp olive oil
- 1 tsp ground cumin
- 1/2 tsp paprika
- Salt and pepper to taste
- 1/4 cup vegetable broth or water
- Fresh parsley, chopped (for garnish)

Step-by-Step Directions:

1. Prepare the Bell Peppers: I'll start by preheating the oven to 375°F (190°C). While the oven is heating up, I'll prepare the bell peppers by cutting off the tops and removing the seeds. I'll then place the peppers upright in a baking dish, making sure they're ready to be stuffed.
2. Cook the Filling: Next, I'll heat the olive oil in a large skillet over medium heat. I'll add the chopped onion and cook until it's soft and translucent, which should take about 5 minutes. After that, I'll add the minced garlic and cook for another minute, just until fragrant.
3. I'll then stir in the cumin and paprika, letting the spices cook for 30 seconds to release their flavors. Now it's time to add the cooked lentils and chopped spinach. I'll season with salt and pepper, and stir everything together until the spinach is wilted and the lentils are heated through.
4. To keep the filling moist, I'll pour in the vegetable broth or water and stir for another minute or two, until the liquid is mostly absorbed.
5. Stuff the Peppers:I'll carefully spoon the lentil and spinach mixture into each of the prepared bell peppers, filling them to the top. If there's any extra filling, I can scatter it around the peppers in the baking dish.
6. Bake the Peppers: I'll cover the dish with foil and bake the stuffed peppers in the preheated oven for 25-30 minutes, or until the peppers are tender but still hold their shape. If you prefer a slightly charred top, I can remove the foil during the last 5 minutes of baking.
7. Serve: Once the peppers are done, I'll remove them from the oven and let them cool slightly. Before serving, I'll sprinkle some freshly chopped parsley on top for a burst of color and freshness.

Nutritional Information (Per Serving):

- Calories: 220 | Protein: 10g | Fiber: 8g | Healthy Fats: 7g | Carbs: 30g

Tips:

1. Make It Ahead: The lentil and spinach filling can be prepared the night before and stored in the fridge. In the morning, all I'll need to do is stuff the peppers and bake them.
2. Add Protein: For an extra protein boost, I can add some crumbled tofu or cooked ground turkey to the lentil mixture.
3. Storage: These stuffed peppers store well in the fridge for up to 3 days, making them a great option for meal prepping.

DINNER RECIPES
Baked Cod with Turmeric and Coconut Milk Sauce
Gluten-Free, Dairy-Free, Soy-Free, Nut-Free

This Baked Cod with Turmeric and Coconut Milk Sauce is one of my favorite dinner recipes because it's light, flavorful, and incredibly nourishing. The cod provides lean protein, while the turmeric and coconut milk create a rich, anti-inflammatory sauce that's both comforting and healthy. This dish aligns perfectly with the Good Energy principles, focusing on balanced nutrition and metabolic health, making it a wonderful choice for a satisfying and health-supportive dinner.

Prep time: 10 minutes | Cooking time: 25 minutes | Servings: 4

Ingredients:

- For the Cod:
- 4 cod fillets (about 6 ounces each)
- 1 tablespoon extra-virgin olive oil
- 1/2 teaspoon sea salt
- 1/4 teaspoon black pepper
- For the Turmeric Coconut Milk Sauce:
- 1 tablespoon extra-virgin olive oil
- 1 small onion, finely chopped
- 2 cloves garlic, minced
- 1 tablespoon fresh ginger, grated
- 1 teaspoon ground turmeric
- 1/2 teaspoon ground cumin
- 1/2 teaspoon ground coriander
- 1/4 teaspoon cayenne pepper (optional, for heat)
- 1 can (13.5 ounces) full-fat coconut milk
- Juice of 1 lime
- 1/4 cup fresh cilantro, chopped (for garnish)

Step-by-Step Directions:

1. Preheat the Oven: I start by preheating the oven to 375°F (190°C). While the oven is heating, I prepare the cod fillets by brushing them with extra-virgin olive oil and seasoning both sides with sea salt and black pepper.
2. Bake the Cod: I place the seasoned cod fillets in a baking dish lined with parchment paper. I bake the cod for about 15-18 minutes, or until it's opaque and flakes easily with a fork. While the cod is baking, I prepare the turmeric coconut milk sauce.
3. Prepare the Sauce: In a large skillet, I heat the olive oil over medium heat. I add the chopped onion and sauté for about 5 minutes until it's soft and translucent. Next, I add the minced garlic and grated ginger, cooking for another 1-2 minutes until fragrant.
4. Add the Spices: I stir in the ground turmeric, cumin, coriander, and cayenne pepper (if using). I let the spices cook for about 1 minute to release their flavors, making sure the sauce has a deep, rich taste.
5. Simmer the Sauce: I pour the coconut milk into the skillet, stirring to combine it with the spices and onion mixture. I bring the sauce to a gentle simmer and let it cook for about 5 minutes, allowing the flavors to meld together. Just before serving, I stir in the fresh lime juice to add a bright, tangy note to the sauce.
6. Serve the Cod: Once the cod is done baking, I carefully transfer the fillets to serving plates. I generously spoon the turmeric coconut milk sauce over each fillet, letting it cascade over the sides. I finish the dish with a sprinkle of fresh cilantro for a burst of color and flavor.

Nutritional Information (Per Serving):

- Calories: 380 | Protein: 28g | Fiber: 3g | Healthy Fats: 28g | Carbs: 7g

Tips:

1. You can add some sautéed spinach or steamed broccoli to the dish for extra nutrients and a splash of green.
2. The turmeric coconut milk sauce can be made ahead of time and stored in the fridge for up to 3 days.

Spaghetti Squash with Walnut Pesto and Grilled Chicken

Gluten-Free, Soy-Free

This is one of my favorite dinners when I'm looking for something hearty yet light. The spaghetti squash serves as a nutritious, low-carb alternative to pasta, while the walnut pesto adds a rich, nutty flavor packed with healthy fats and antioxidants. The grilled chicken provides a satisfying source of lean protein, making this dish a well-rounded meal that supports metabolic health and reduces inflammation.

Prep time: 15 minutes | Cooking time: 45 minutes | Servings: 4

Ingredients:

- For the Spaghetti Squash:
- 1 large spaghetti squash, halved and seeds removed
- 1 tablespoon extra-virgin olive oil
- 1/2 teaspoon sea salt
- 1/4 teaspoon black pepper
- For the Walnut Pesto:
- 1 cup fresh basil leaves
- 1/2 cup walnuts
- 1/4 cup extra-virgin olive oil
- 2 cloves garlic, minced
- 2 tablespoons fresh lemon juice (about 1 lemon)
- 1/4 teaspoon sea salt
- 1/4 teaspoon black pepper
- 2 tablespoons nutritional yeast (optional, for a cheesy flavor)
- For the Grilled Chicken:
- 1 pound chicken breasts, boneless and skinless
- 1 tablespoon extra-virgin olive oil
- 1/2 teaspoon sea salt
- 1/4 teaspoon black pepper
- 1/2 teaspoon dried oregano

Step-by-Step Directions:

1. Roast the Spaghetti Squash: I start by preheating the oven to 400°F (200°C). I drizzle the cut sides of the spaghetti squash with olive oil, then sprinkle with sea salt and black pepper. I place the squash halves cut-side down on a baking sheet lined with parchment paper. I roast the squash for about 35-40 minutes, or until it's tender and easily pulls into spaghetti-like strands with a fork.
2. Prepare the Walnut Pesto: While the squash is roasting, I make the walnut pesto. In a food processor, I combine the fresh basil leaves, walnuts, garlic, lemon juice, sea salt, and black pepper. I pulse a few times to break down the ingredients. With the processor running, I slowly drizzle in the olive oil until the pesto reaches a smooth consistency. If you're using nutritional yeast, add it at this stage for an extra burst of flavor.
3. Grill the Chicken: As the pesto is coming together, I season the chicken breasts with olive oil, sea salt, black pepper, and dried oregano. I heat a grill pan over medium heat (you can also use an outdoor grill) and cook the chicken for about 6-7 minutes on each side, or until it's cooked through and has nice grill marks. Once done, I let the chicken rest for a few minutes before slicing it into strips.
4. Assemble the Dish: Once the spaghetti squash is ready, I use a fork to gently scrape the flesh into long strands, keeping it inside the squash shell if I want to serve it this way. I toss the squash strands with the walnut pesto until they're well coated. I then divide the squash among four plates or leave it in the squash shells for a fun presentation. I top each serving with the grilled chicken slices.
5. Serve and Enjoy: I garnish the dish with a few extra basil leaves and a sprinkle of walnuts if desired. This meal is best enjoyed warm and is both comforting and full of flavor.

Nutritional Information (Per Serving): Calories: 480 | Protein: 35g | Fiber: 6g | Healthy Fats: 32g | Carbs: 18g

Tips:

1. If you prefer a plant-based version, you can substitute the grilled chicken with grilled tofu or tempeh.

Grass-Fed Beef Stir-Fry with Broccoli and Cauliflower Rice

Gluten-Free, Dairy-Free, Soy-Free, Nut-Free

This Grass-Fed Beef Stir-Fry with Broccoli and Cauliflower Rice is one of my go-to dinners when I want something quick, nutritious, and satisfying. The grass-fed beef provides high-quality protein and essential fatty acids, while the broccoli and cauliflower rice pack in fiber and antioxidants. This dish is designed to support metabolic health, reduce inflammation, and offer balanced nutrition, making it a perfect example of a Good Energy meal.

Prep time: 15 minutes | Cooking time: 20 minutes | Servings: 4

Ingredients:

- For the Stir-Fry:
- 1 pound grass-fed beef sirloin or flank steak, thinly sliced
- 1 tablespoon extra-virgin olive oil (or avocado oil)
- 3 cups broccoli florets
- 1 red bell pepper, thinly sliced
- 3 cloves garlic, minced
- 1 tablespoon fresh ginger, grated
- 2 tablespoons coconut aminos (or tamari for soy-free option)
- 1 tablespoon rice vinegar
- 1/2 teaspoon sea salt
- 1/4 teaspoon black pepper
- 1/4 teaspoon red pepper flakes (optional, for heat)
- For the Cauliflower Rice:
- 1 medium head of cauliflower, riced (or 4 cups pre-riced cauliflower)
- 1 tablespoon extra-virgin olive oil (or avocado oil)
- 1/4 teaspoon sea salt
- 1/4 teaspoon black pepper
- 1 tablespoon fresh cilantro, chopped (for garnish, optional)

Step-by-Step Directions:

1. Prepare the Cauliflower Rice: I start by ricing the cauliflower if I'm using a whole head. I do this by chopping the cauliflower into florets and pulsing them in a food processor until they resemble rice grains. Then, I heat the olive oil in a large skillet over medium heat. I add the riced cauliflower, sea salt, and black pepper, and sauté for about 5-7 minutes until the cauliflower is tender. Once done, I set it aside and keep it warm.
2. Cook the Beef: In another large skillet or wok, I heat the olive oil over medium-high heat. Once hot, I add the thinly sliced beef and cook for about 3-4 minutes until it's browned on all sides. I remove the beef from the skillet and set it aside, leaving any juices in the pan.
3. Stir-Fry the Vegetables: In the same skillet, I add the minced garlic and grated ginger, cooking for about 1 minute until fragrant. I then add the broccoli florets and red bell pepper, stirring frequently, and cook for about 5 minutes until the vegetables are tender-crisp.
4. Combine and Finish the Stir-Fry: I return the cooked beef to the skillet with the vegetables. I add the coconut aminos, rice vinegar, sea salt, black pepper, and red pepper flakes (if using). I stir everything together, cooking for another 2-3 minutes until the flavors are well combined and the beef is heated through.
5. Serve and Enjoy: I serve the beef stir-fry over the cauliflower rice, garnishing with fresh cilantro if desired. This meal is best enjoyed immediately while it's hot and full of flavor.

Nutritional Information (Per Serving): Calories: 350 | Protein: 28g | Fiber: 6g | Healthy Fats: 18g | Carbs: 12g

Tips:

1. Make It Your Own: Feel free to add other vegetables like snap peas, zucchini, or carrots to the stir-fry for added variety and nutrition.
2. Prep Ahead: The beef can be marinated in the coconut aminos and rice vinegar for extra flavor if you have time. Simply let it sit in the marinade for 30 minutes before cooking.

Lemon-Herb Grilled Tofu with Quinoa Pilaf

Gluten-Free, Dairy-Free, Soy-Free

This is a vibrant and nourishing dinner that I often turn to when I want a plant-based meal that's full of flavor and balanced nutrition. The tofu is marinated in a zesty lemon-herb mixture that infuses it with bright, refreshing flavors, while the quinoa pilaf provides a protein-packed, fiber-rich base.

Prep time: 15 minutes | Cooking time: 30 minutes | Servings: 4

Ingredients:

- For the Lemon-Herb Grilled Tofu:
- 1 block (14 ounces) firm tofu, pressed and sliced into 1-inch thick slabs
- 1/4 cup fresh lemon juice (about 2 lemons)
- 2 tablespoons extra-virgin olive oil
- 2 cloves garlic, minced
- 1 tablespoon fresh thyme leaves, chopped
- 1 tablespoon fresh rosemary, chopped
- 1 tablespoon fresh parsley, chopped
- 1/2 teaspoon sea salt
- 1/4 teaspoon black pepper

- For the Quinoa Pilaf:
- 1 cup quinoa, rinsed
- 2 cups vegetable broth (or water)
- 1 small onion, finely chopped
- 1 carrot, diced
- 1 stalk celery, diced
- 1 tablespoon extra-virgin olive oil
- 1 clove garlic, minced
- 1/4 teaspoon sea salt
- 1/4 teaspoon black pepper
- 1/4 cup fresh parsley, chopped (for garnish)

Step-by-Step Directions:

1. Marinate the Tofu: I start by preparing the marinade for the tofu. In a small mixing bowl, I whisk together the fresh lemon juice, olive oil, minced garlic, thyme, rosemary, parsley, sea salt, and black pepper. I place the tofu slabs in a shallow dish and pour the marinade over them, making sure each piece is well-coated. I let the tofu marinate for at least 15 minutes, turning once to ensure even flavor absorption.
2. Cook the Quinoa Pilaf: While the tofu is marinating, I begin the quinoa pilaf. I heat the olive oil in a medium saucepan over medium heat. I add the chopped onion, carrot, and celery, sautéing for about 5 minutes until the vegetables are softened. Next, I stir in the minced garlic and cook for another minute until fragrant. I add the rinsed quinoa and stir to coat it with the oil and vegetables.
3. Simmer the Quinoa: I pour the vegetable broth into the saucepan with the quinoa and bring it to a boil. Once boiling, I reduce the heat to low, cover the pot, and let the quinoa simmer for about 15 minutes, or until the quinoa is tender and the liquid is absorbed. I fluff the quinoa with a fork and season it with sea salt and black pepper to taste.
4. Grill the Tofu: While the quinoa is cooking, I heat a grill pan over medium-high heat (you can also use an outdoor grill). I remove the tofu from the marinade and place it on the hot grill. I cook the tofu for about 4-5 minutes on each side, until it has nice grill marks and is heated through. The lemon-herb marinade caramelizes slightly, adding a wonderful depth of flavor to the tofu.
5. Assemble the Dish: I serve the grilled tofu over a bed of quinoa pilaf, garnishing with fresh parsley for an added burst of freshness. The combination of the zesty tofu and the savory quinoa pilaf makes for a satisfying and balanced meal.

Nutritional Information (Per Serving): Calories: 320 | Protein: 15g | Fiber: 6g | Healthy Fats: 16g | Carbs: 30g

Tips:

1. Press the Tofu: To get the best texture, I always press the tofu to remove excess moisture before marinating. This helps the tofu absorb more of the marinade and improves its texture when grilled.
2. Add Extra Veggies: You can easily add more vegetables to the quinoa pilaf, such as diced zucchini or bell peppers, for added flavor and nutrients.

Braised Lamb Shanks with Root Vegetables

Gluten-Free, Dairy-Free, Soy-Free, Nut-Free

Braised Lamb Shanks with Root Vegetables is a deeply satisfying and nourishing dinner that's perfect for cooler evenings when you want something hearty and full of flavor. The lamb shanks are slowly braised until tender, absorbing the rich flavors of the broth and root vegetables. This dish is rich in protein, healthy fats, and a variety of vitamins and minerals, making it an excellent choice for supporting metabolic health and reducing inflammation.

Prep time: 20 minutes | Cooking time: 2.5 to 3 hours| Servings: 4

Ingredients:

- For the Braised Lamb Shanks:
- 4 lamb shanks (about 1.5 pounds each)
- 2 tablespoons extra-virgin olive oil
- 1 large onion, chopped
- 4 cloves garlic, minced
- 2 large carrots, chopped into 1-inch pieces
- 2 parsnips, chopped into 1-inch pieces
- 2 sweet potatoes, peeled and chopped into 1-inch pieces
- 1 cup celery, chopped
- 2 cups beef broth (or bone broth)
- 1 cup red wine (optional, or use more broth)
- 1 can (14.5 ounces) diced tomatoes
- 2 sprigs fresh rosemary
- 2 sprigs fresh thyme
- 2 bay leaves
- 1 teaspoon sea salt
- 1/2 teaspoon black pepper

Step-by-Step Directions:

1. Sear the Lamb Shanks: I start by preheating my oven to 325°F (160°C). In a large, oven-safe pot or Dutch oven, I heat the olive oil over medium-high heat. I season the lamb shanks generously with sea salt and black pepper, then sear them in the hot oil, turning to brown on all sides. This takes about 8-10 minutes. Once browned, I remove the lamb shanks from the pot and set them aside.
2. Sauté the Aromatics: In the same pot, I add the chopped onion, garlic, carrots, parsnips, sweet potatoes, and celery. I sauté the vegetables for about 5 minutes, or until they start to soften and the onion becomes translucent. This step helps to build the flavor base for the braise.
3. Deglaze the Pot: Next, I pour in the red wine (if using) to deglaze the pot, scraping up any browned bits from the bottom with a wooden spoon. I let the wine simmer for about 2 minutes to reduce slightly. If you're skipping the wine, you can deglaze with a bit of the beef broth.
4. Add the Braising Liquid: I then add the beef broth, diced tomatoes (with their juice), rosemary, thyme, and bay leaves to the pot. I stir everything together, then return the lamb shanks to the pot, nestling them among the vegetables. I bring the mixture to a gentle simmer on the stovetop.
5. Braise in the Oven: Once simmering, I cover the pot with a lid and transfer it to the preheated oven. I let the lamb shanks braise for 2.5 to 3 hours, or until the meat is tender and easily pulls away from the bone. During this time, the flavors will meld beautifully, creating a rich and savory dish.
6. I carefully remove the lamb shanks from the pot and serve them on a platter with the braised vegetables and some of the flavorful sauce spooned over the top. This dish is best enjoyed hot, straight from the oven.

Nutritional Information (Per Serving):

- Calories: 650 | Protein: 40g | Fiber: 8g | Healthy Fats: 35g | Carbs: 30g

Tips:

1. Make It Ahead: This dish tastes even better the next day, as the flavors continue to develop. Simply store the leftovers in the fridge and reheat gently before serving.
2. Use Bone Broth: For an extra nutritional boost, use homemade bone broth in place of regular beef broth. It adds even more depth of flavor and health benefits.

Lemon and Herb Baked Chicken with Brussels Sprouts

Gluten-Free, Dairy-Free, Soy-Free, Nut-Free

This Lemon and Herb Baked Chicken with Brussels Sprouts is a simple yet flavorful dinner that's perfect for those nights when you want something healthy and satisfying. The chicken is marinated in a zesty lemon and herb mixture, which infuses it with bright flavors while keeping it juicy and tender. Paired with roasted Brussels sprouts, this dish is rich in vitamins, minerals, and healthy fats, making it a perfect choice for supporting metabolic health and reducing inflammation.

Prep time: 15 minutes | Cooking time: 35 minutes | Servings: 4

Ingredients:

- For the Lemon and Herb Chicken:
- 4 boneless, skinless chicken breasts (about 6 ounces each)
- 1/4 cup fresh lemon juice (about 2 lemons)
- 2 tablespoons extra-virgin olive oil
- 3 cloves garlic, minced
- 1 tablespoon fresh rosemary, chopped
- 1 tablespoon fresh thyme, chopped
- 1 tablespoon fresh parsley, chopped
- 1 teaspoon sea salt
- 1/2 teaspoon black pepper
- Lemon slices, for garnish (optional)
- For the Roasted Brussels Sprouts:
- 4 cups Brussels sprouts, trimmed and halved
- 2 tablespoons extra-virgin olive oil
- 1/2 teaspoon sea salt
- 1/4 teaspoon black pepper
- 1 teaspoon fresh lemon zest (optional, for extra flavor)

Step-by-Step Directions:

1. Marinate the Chicken: I begin by preparing the marinade for the chicken. In a large mixing bowl, I whisk together the fresh lemon juice, olive oil, minced garlic, rosemary, thyme, parsley, sea salt, and black pepper. I then add the chicken breasts to the bowl, turning them to coat evenly in the marinade. I let the chicken marinate for at least 15 minutes at room temperature or up to 2 hours in the refrigerator for more intense flavor.
2. Preheat the Oven: While the chicken is marinating, I preheat my oven to 400°F (200°C). I also prepare a large baking sheet by lining it with parchment paper.
3. Roast the Brussels Sprouts: I place the halved Brussels sprouts on the prepared baking sheet. I drizzle them with olive oil and sprinkle with sea salt and black pepper. I toss the sprouts to ensure they're evenly coated, then spread them out in a single layer. I roast the Brussels sprouts in the preheated oven for about 20-25 minutes, or until they're tender and slightly caramelized on the edges.
4. Bake the Chicken: While the Brussels sprouts are roasting, I transfer the marinated chicken breasts to another baking dish, arranging them in a single layer. I pour any remaining marinade over the top of the chicken. I bake the chicken in the oven alongside the Brussels sprouts for about 20-25 minutes, or until the chicken is cooked through and reaches an internal temperature of 165°F (75°C). If desired, I garnish the chicken with lemon slices for a touch of brightness.
5. Serve and Enjoy: I plate the lemon and herb baked chicken with a generous serving of roasted Brussels sprouts. The combination of the juicy, flavorful chicken and the crispy, caramelized Brussels sprouts makes this a delightful and balanced dinner.

Nutritional Information (Per Serving): Calories: 350 | Protein: 35g | Fiber: 6g | Healthy Fats: 18g | Carbs: 14g

Tips:

1. For even more flavor, I sometimes add a pinch of red pepper flakes to the marinade for a bit of heat.
2. Meal Prep: This dish is great for meal prep. The chicken and Brussels sprouts can be stored in the fridge for up to 3 days and reheated for a quick and easy meal.

Roasted Butternut Squash and Quinoa Pilaf with Cranberries

Gluten-Free, Dairy-Free, Soy-Free, Nut-Free

This Roasted Butternut Squash and Quinoa Pilaf with Cranberries is a delightful, nutritious dinner option that's perfect for a cozy evening. The roasted butternut squash adds a natural sweetness and is packed with vitamins and antioxidants, while the quinoa provides a complete protein source, making this dish both hearty and healthful. The addition of cranberries adds a tart contrast that brightens the dish.

Prep time: 15 minutes | Cooking time: 35 minutes | Servings: 4

Ingredients:

- For the Roasted Butternut Squash:
- 1 medium butternut squash, peeled, seeded, and diced into 1-inch cubes
- 2 tablespoons extra-virgin olive oil
- 1/2 teaspoon sea salt
- 1/4 teaspoon black pepper
- 1/2 teaspoon ground cinnamon
- For the Quinoa Pilaf:
- 1 cup quinoa, rinsed
- 2 cups vegetable broth (or water)
- 1 small onion, finely chopped
- 2 cloves garlic, minced
- 1/4 cup dried cranberries (unsweetened if possible)
- 2 tablespoons extra-virgin olive oil
- 1/2 teaspoon sea salt
- 1/4 teaspoon black pepper
- 1/4 cup fresh parsley, chopped (for garnish)

Step-by-Step Directions:

1. Roast the Butternut Squash: I start by preheating the oven to 400°F (200°C). I place the diced butternut squash on a large baking sheet, drizzle with the olive oil, and sprinkle with sea salt, black pepper, and ground cinnamon. I toss the squash to coat evenly, then spread it out in a single layer. I roast the squash for about 25-30 minutes, or until it's tender and caramelized on the edges, turning once halfway through the cooking time.
2. Cook the Quinoa: While the squash is roasting, I heat 1 tablespoon of olive oil in a medium saucepan over medium heat. I add the chopped onion and sauté for about 5 minutes until it becomes soft and translucent. Then, I add the minced garlic and cook for another minute until fragrant.
3. Simmer the Quinoa: I stir in the rinsed quinoa, coating it with the oil, onion, and garlic mixture. I then pour in the vegetable broth, bringing it to a boil. Once boiling, I reduce the heat to low, cover the pot, and let the quinoa simmer for about 15 minutes, or until all the liquid is absorbed and the quinoa is tender. After cooking, I fluff the quinoa with a fork and stir in the dried cranberries, allowing them to soften in the warm quinoa.
4. Once the butternut squash is roasted, I gently fold it into the cooked quinoa mixture. The roasted squash adds a sweet, nutty flavor that complements the tart cranberries and the savory quinoa perfectly.
5. Serve and Enjoy: I serve the Roasted Butternut Squash and Quinoa Pilaf warm, garnished with fresh parsley for a pop of color and added freshness. This dish is hearty enough to be a main course but light enough to leave you feeling energized.

Nutritional Information (Per Serving):

- Calories: 380 | Protein: 8g | Fiber: 7g | Healthy Fats: 14g | Carbs: 56g

Tips:

1. Make It Ahead: The quinoa pilaf can be made ahead of time and reheated gently before serving. This makes it a great option for meal prepping or a quick weeknight dinner.
2. Add More Veggies: Feel free to add other roasted vegetables like Brussels sprouts or carrots to the pilaf for added flavor and nutrients.

Herb-Crusted Cod with Garlic Green Beans

Gluten-Free, Dairy-Free, Soy-Free, Nut-Free

This Herb-Crusted Cod with Garlic Green Beans is a light yet satisfying dinner option that's perfect for a nutritious, balanced meal. The cod is coated in a flavorful herb mixture and baked until perfectly tender, while the garlic green beans add a crunchy, savory side that complements the fish beautifully. This dish is rich in lean protein, healthy fats, and antioxidants, supporting metabolic health and reducing inflammation. It's a great example of a Good Energy meal, ensuring you feel nourished and energized.

Prep time: 15 minutes | Cooking time: 20 minutes | Servings: 4

Ingredients:

- For the Herb-Crusted Cod:
- 4 cod fillets (about 6 ounces each)
- 1/4 cup fresh parsley, finely chopped
- 1 tablespoon fresh thyme leaves, chopped
- 1 tablespoon fresh rosemary, chopped
- 2 cloves garlic, minced
- 2 tablespoons extra-virgin olive oil
- 1 teaspoon lemon zest (from 1 lemon)
- 1/2 teaspoon sea salt
- 1/4 teaspoon black pepper
- Lemon wedges, for serving
- For the Garlic Green Beans:
- 1 pound green beans, trimmed
- 1 tablespoon extra-virgin olive oil
- 3 cloves garlic, minced
- 1/4 teaspoon sea salt
- 1/4 teaspoon black pepper
- 1 tablespoon fresh lemon juice

Step-by-Step Directions:

1. Preheat the Oven: I start by preheating my oven to 400°F (200°C). I line a baking sheet with parchment paper to make cleanup easier.
2. Prepare the Herb-Crusted Cod: In a small bowl, I mix together the chopped parsley, thyme, rosemary, minced garlic, lemon zest, sea salt, and black pepper. I then stir in the olive oil until the mixture forms a coarse paste. I place the cod fillets on the prepared baking sheet. Using my hands, I evenly press the herb mixture onto the top of each cod fillet, ensuring that each piece is well-coated.
3. Bake the Cod: I bake the cod in the preheated oven for 12-15 minutes, or until the fish is opaque and flakes easily with a fork. While the cod is baking, I prepare the garlic green beans.
4. Cook the Garlic Green Beans: In a large skillet, I heat the olive oil over medium heat. I add the minced garlic and sauté for about 1 minute until it's fragrant but not browned. Then, I add the green beans, tossing them to coat in the garlic oil. I cook the green beans for about 5-7 minutes, stirring occasionally, until they are tender-crisp. Just before serving, I drizzle the green beans with fresh lemon juice and season with sea salt and black pepper to taste.
5. Serve and Enjoy: I serve the herb-crusted cod fillets alongside the garlic green beans, garnished with lemon wedges for an extra burst of citrus flavor. This dish is best enjoyed immediately while the fish is flaky and the green beans are still crisp.

Nutritional Information (Per Serving):

- Calories: 310 | Protein: 32g | Fiber: 5g | Healthy Fats: 14g | Carbs: 10g

Tips:

1. Make It Extra Crispy: For an added crunch, you can sprinkle the herb-crusted cod with a bit of gluten-free breadcrumbs before baking.
2. Use Fresh Herbs: Fresh herbs really make a difference in this dish, so I recommend using fresh rather than dried if possible.

Moroccan-Spiced Lamb with Cauliflower Couscous

Gluten-Free, Dairy-Free, Soy-Free, Nut-Free

This dish is crafted to support metabolic health and provide balanced nutrition, making it a perfect example of a Good Energy meal. It's a great option for a dinner that feels indulgent but is packed with nutrients.

Prep time: 20 minutes | Cooking time: 40 minutes | Servings: 4

Ingredients:

- For the Moroccan-Spiced Lamb:
- 1.5 pounds lamb shoulder or leg, cut into 1-inch cubes
- 2 tablespoons extra-virgin olive oil
- 1 large onion, finely chopped
- 3 cloves garlic, minced
- 1 tablespoon ground cumin
- 1 tablespoon ground coriander
- 1 teaspoon ground cinnamon
- 1 teaspoon ground turmeric
- 1/2 teaspoon ground ginger
- 1/2 teaspoon paprika
- 1/4 teaspoon cayenne pepper (optional, for heat)
- 1 teaspoon sea salt
- 1/2 teaspoon black pepper
- 1 cup canned diced tomatoes, with juices
- 1/2 cup water or bone broth
- 2 tablespoons fresh parsley, chopped (for garnish)
- 2 tablespoons fresh cilantro, chopped (for garnish)
- For the Cauliflower Couscous:
- 1 medium head of cauliflower, riced (about 4 cups)
- 2 tablespoons extra-virgin olive oil
- 1/2 teaspoon sea salt
- 1/4 teaspoon black pepper
- 1/4 teaspoon ground turmeric (optional, for color)
- 1/4 cup golden raisins (optional, for sweetness)
- 2 tablespoons fresh mint, chopped (for garnish)

Step-by-Step Directions:

1. Prepare the Moroccan-Spiced Lamb: I start by heating the olive oil in a large pot or Dutch oven over medium heat. I add the chopped onion and sauté for about 5 minutes until it becomes soft and translucent. Then, I stir in the minced garlic and cook for another minute until fragrant.
2. Season and Brown the Lamb: I add the lamb cubes to the pot, searing them on all sides until they are browned. This takes about 5-7 minutes. Once the lamb is browned, I stir in the ground cumin, coriander, cinnamon, turmeric, ginger, paprika, cayenne pepper (if using), sea salt, and black pepper. I mix everything well, letting the spices coat the lamb evenly.
3. Simmer the Lamb: I add the diced tomatoes (with their juices) and water or bone broth to the pot, stirring to combine. I bring the mixture to a simmer, then reduce the heat to low. I cover the pot and let the lamb cook gently for about 30-35 minutes, or until it's tender and infused with the rich, Moroccan spices.
4. Prepare the Cauliflower Couscous: While the lamb is simmering, I prepare the cauliflower couscous. I rice the cauliflower by pulsing florets in a food processor until they resemble couscous grains. Then, I heat the olive oil in a large skillet over medium heat. I add the riced cauliflower, sea salt, black pepper, and ground turmeric (if using). I sauté the cauliflower for about 5-7 minutes until it's tender but not mushy. If you like a touch of sweetness, you can stir in the golden raisins during the last minute of cooking.
5. Serve and Enjoy: I plate the Moroccan-Spiced Lamb over the cauliflower couscous, garnishing with fresh parsley, cilantro, and mint. The combination of warm spices, tender lamb, and light cauliflower couscous makes this dish both comforting and refreshing.

Nutritional Information (Per Serving):

- Calories: 450 | Protein: 30g | Fiber: 6g | Healthy Fats: 28g | Carbs: 18g

Turkey Meatballs in Tomato Basil Sauce over Spaghetti Squash

Gluten-Free, Dairy-Free, Soy-Free, Nut-Free

Served over spaghetti squash, a low-carb alternative to traditional pasta, this dish aligns perfectly with the Good Energy principles, ensuring a balanced meal that promotes vitality.

Prep time: 20 minutes | Cooking time: 45 minutes | Servings: 4

Ingredients:

- For the Turkey Meatballs:
- 1 pound ground turkey
- 1/4 cup gluten-free breadcrumbs (or almond flour for grain-free)
- 1 egg
- 2 cloves garlic, minced
- 1/4 cup fresh parsley, chopped
- 1/4 cup fresh basil, chopped
- 1 teaspoon dried oregano
- 1/2 teaspoon sea salt
- 1/4 teaspoon black pepper
- 1 tablespoon extra-virgin olive oil (for browning)
- For the Tomato Basil Sauce:
- 1 tablespoon extra-virgin olive oil
- 1 small onion, finely chopped
- 3 cloves garlic, minced
- 1 can (28 ounces) crushed tomatoes
- 1/4 cup fresh basil, chopped
- 1 teaspoon dried oregano
- 1/2 teaspoon sea salt
- 1/4 teaspoon black pepper
- 1/2 teaspoon red pepper flakes (optional, for a bit of heat)
- For the Spaghetti Squash:
- 1 large spaghetti squash
- 1 tablespoon extra-virgin olive oil
- 1/2 teaspoon sea salt
- 1/4 teaspoon black pepper

Step-by-Step Directions:

1. Prepare the Spaghetti Squash: I start by preheating the oven to 400°F (200°C). I carefully slice the spaghetti squash in half lengthwise and scoop out the seeds. I then drizzle the insides with olive oil and sprinkle with sea salt and black pepper. I place the squash halves cut side down on a baking sheet lined with parchment paper and roast for about 35-40 minutes, or until the squash is tender and the strands easily pull away from the skin with a fork.
2. Make the Turkey Meatballs: While the squash is roasting, I prepare the turkey meatballs. In a large mixing bowl, I combine the ground turkey, gluten-free breadcrumbs, egg, minced garlic, parsley, basil, dried oregano, sea salt, and black pepper. I mix everything together with my hands until just combined, being careful not to overwork the meat. I then form the mixture into 1-inch meatballs. In a large skillet, I heat the olive oil over medium heat and brown the meatballs on all sides, about 5 minutes total. I remove the browned meatballs from the skillet and set them aside.
3. Prepare the Tomato Basil Sauce: In the same skillet, I heat the olive oil over medium heat. I add the chopped onion and sauté for about 5 minutes until softened. I then add the minced garlic and cook for another minute until fragrant. I pour in the crushed tomatoes, fresh basil, dried oregano, sea salt, black pepper, and red pepper flakes (if using). I stir everything together and bring the sauce to a simmer.
4. Simmer the Meatballs in Sauce: I return the browned meatballs to the skillet with the tomato basil sauce, nestling them into the sauce. I cover the skillet and let the meatballs simmer in the sauce for about 20 minutes, or until they're cooked through and the flavors have melded beautifully.
5. Serve and Enjoy: Once the spaghetti squash is done roasting, I use a fork to scrape out the strands and divide them among serving plates. I spoon the turkey meatballs and tomato basil sauce over the top of the spaghetti squash, garnishing with additional fresh basil if desired. This dish is best enjoyed hot and fresh.

Nutritional Information (Per Serving):

- Calories: 380 | Protein: 30g | Fiber: 7g | Healthy Fats: 18g | Carbs: 28g

Roasted Chicken with Sweet Potatoes and Brussels Sprouts

Gluten-Free, Dairy-Free, Soy-Free, Nut-Free

This Roasted Chicken with Sweet Potatoes and Brussels Sprouts is a balanced and nutritious dinner option that aligns perfectly with the Good Energy principles. The combination of lean protein, complex carbohydrates, and fiber-rich vegetables provides a satisfying meal that supports metabolic health and sustained energy.

Prep time: 15 minutes | Cooking time: 35 minutes | Servings: 4

Ingredients:

- For the Roasted Chicken:
- 4 boneless, skinless chicken breasts
- 1 tbsp olive oil
- 1 tsp garlic powder
- 1 tsp paprika
- Salt and pepper to taste
- For the Roasted Vegetables:

- 2 large sweet potatoes, peeled and cubed
- 2 cups Brussels sprouts, halved
- 1 tbsp olive oil
- 1 tsp dried rosemary
- 1/2 tsp ground cumin
- Salt and pepper to taste

Step-by-Step Directions:

1. Preheat the Oven:I'll start by preheating the oven to 400°F (200°C). This temperature is ideal for roasting both the chicken and vegetables, ensuring they cook evenly and develop a nice, caramelized exterior.
2. Prepare the Chicken:While the oven is heating up, I'll place the chicken breasts on a baking sheet lined with parchment paper. I'll drizzle them with olive oil and then season with garlic powder, paprika, salt, and pepper. I'll make sure to rub the seasoning evenly on all sides for full flavor.
3. Prepare the Vegetables:On a separate baking sheet, I'll spread out the cubed sweet potatoes and halved Brussels sprouts. I'll drizzle them with olive oil and sprinkle on the rosemary, cumin, salt, and pepper. I'll toss everything together so the veggies are well-coated with the seasoning.
4. Roast Everything:I'll place both baking sheets in the preheated oven—one with the chicken and the other with the vegetables. I'll roast the chicken for about 25-30 minutes, or until it reaches an internal temperature of 165°F (74°C) and the juices run clear. The vegetables will take around 30-35 minutes, or until they are tender and golden brown, with a slight crispiness on the edges.
5. Rest and Serve:Once everything is cooked, I'll remove the chicken from the oven and let it rest for 5 minutes before slicing. This resting time helps the juices redistribute, making the chicken moist and flavorful. I'll then plate the chicken slices alongside the roasted sweet potatoes and Brussels sprouts, ready to serve.
6. Tips:Make It Ahead: This dish can be prepped the night before. I'll marinate the chicken and chop the vegetables in advance, storing them in the fridge. In the morning, all I need to do is roast them.
7. Add Some Greens: If I want to add more variety, I can serve this with a side of fresh greens like arugula or spinach.
8. Storage: Leftovers can be stored in an airtight container in the fridge for up to 3 days, making it a great option for meal prep.

Nutritional Information (Per Serving):

- Calories: 350 | Protein: 30g | Fiber: 6g | Healthy Fats: 12g | Carbs: 28g

Serving Suggestions:

- This dish pairs well with a simple mixed greens salad or a refreshing cucumber and lemon water to complement the flavors. It's a filling dinner that's great on its own, but you can also serve it with a side of avocado slices for an extra boost of healthy fats.

Lemon-Garlic Shrimp with Zucchini Noodles

Gluten-Free, Dairy-Free, Soy-Free, Nut-Free

This Lemon-Garlic Shrimp with Zucchini Noodles recipe is a refreshing and light dinner option that aligns with the Good Energy principles. The combination of protein-rich shrimp and nutrient-dense zucchini noodles offers a low-carb, high-protein meal that supports metabolic health and provides sustained energy.

Prep time: 15 minutes | Cooking time: 10 minutes | Servings: 2

Ingredients:

- For the Shrimp:
- 10 oz shrimp, peeled and deveined
- 1 tbsp olive oil
- 2 cloves garlic, minced
- Zest and juice of 1 lemon
- Salt and pepper to taste
- 1/4 tsp red pepper flakes (optional for a bit of heat)
- For the Zucchini Noodles:
- 2 medium zucchinis, spiralized into noodles
- 1 tbsp olive oil
- Salt and pepper to taste

Step-by-Step Directions:

1. Prepare the Zucchini Noodles: I'll start by spiralizing the zucchinis into noodles using a spiralizer. If you don't have a spiralizer, you can also use a vegetable peeler to create thin ribbons. I'll then set the noodles aside while preparing the shrimp.
2. Cook the Shrimp: In a large skillet, I'll heat the olive oil over medium heat. Once hot, I'll add the minced garlic and sauté for about 1 minute, until it's fragrant but not browned.
3. Next, I'll add the shrimp to the skillet, seasoning with salt, pepper, and red pepper flakes if using. I'll cook the shrimp for about 2-3 minutes on each side until they are pink and opaque.
4. Just before the shrimp are done, I'll add the lemon zest and juice to the skillet, stirring to coat the shrimp evenly. I'll then remove the shrimp from the skillet and set them aside.
5. Cook the Zucchini Noodles: In the same skillet, I'll add another tablespoon of olive oil and toss in the zucchini noodles. I'll sauté them for 2-3 minutes until they are just tender but still have a slight crunch. I'll season them with a pinch of salt and pepper.
6. Combine and Serve: I'll divide the zucchini noodles between two plates and top them with the lemon-garlic shrimp. I'll drizzle any remaining lemon-garlic sauce from the skillet over the top for extra flavor.
7. To finish, I'll garnish the dish with a sprinkle of fresh parsley or extra lemon zest if desired.

Tips:

1. Zucchini Alternatives: If you prefer, you can use spaghetti squash or carrot noodles as an alternative to zucchini noodles.
2. Extra Veggies: Feel free to add other quick-cooking vegetables like cherry tomatoes or spinach to the dish for added color and nutrients.
3. Storage: This dish is best served fresh but can be stored in an airtight container in the refrigerator for up to 1 day.

Nutritional Information (Per Serving):

- Calories: 280 | Protein: 28g | Fiber: 4g | Healthy Fats: 14g | Carbs: 10g

Stuffed Portobello Mushrooms with Quinoa and Spinach

Gluten-Free, Dairy-Free, Soy-Free

This Stuffed Portobello Mushrooms with Quinoa and Spinach recipe is a nourishing dinner option packed with protein, fiber, and healthy fats. It aligns perfectly with the Good Energy principles, focusing on balanced nutrition and anti-inflammatory ingredients. The combination of hearty mushrooms, quinoa, and spinach provides a satisfying meal that supports metabolic health and keeps energy levels steady.

Prep time: 15 minutes | Cooking time: 20 minutes | Servings: 2

Ingredients:

- For the Mushrooms:
- 4 large Portobello mushrooms, stems removed and gills scraped out
- 1 tbsp olive oil
- Salt and pepper to taste
- For the Quinoa Filling:
- 1/2 cup quinoa, rinsed
- 1 cup vegetable broth or water
- 1 tbsp olive oil
- 1 small onion, finely chopped
- 2 cloves garlic, minced
- 2 cups fresh spinach, chopped
- 1/4 cup sun-dried tomatoes, chopped (optional)
- Salt and pepper to taste
- 1 tbsp nutritional yeast (optional, for a cheesy flavor)

Step-by-Step Directions:

1. Prepare the Mushrooms: I'll start by preheating the oven to 375°F (190°C). While the oven heats up, I'll brush the Portobello mushrooms with olive oil and season them with salt and pepper. I'll place the mushrooms on a baking sheet, gill side up, and bake for about 10 minutes until they begin to soften. After baking, I'll set them aside to cool slightly.
2. Cook the Quinoa: While the mushrooms are baking, I'll prepare the quinoa. I'll bring the vegetable broth (or water) to a boil in a medium saucepan. I'll then add the quinoa, reduce the heat, cover, and let it simmer for about 15 minutes, or until the quinoa is cooked and the liquid is absorbed. Once the quinoa is done, I'll fluff it with a fork and set it aside.
3. Prepare the Filling :In a large skillet, I'll heat the olive oil over medium heat. I'll then add the chopped onion and sauté it for about 3-4 minutes until it's softened and translucent. Next, I'll add the minced garlic and cook for another minute until fragrant. I'll then add the chopped spinach to the skillet, cooking until wilted. If I'm using sun-dried tomatoes, I'll add them at this stage as well. Finally, I'll stir in the cooked quinoa, season the mixture with salt, pepper, and nutritional yeast (if using), and cook until everything is well combined and heated through.
4. Stuff the Mushrooms: I'll divide the quinoa and spinach filling evenly between the four mushrooms, pressing it down slightly to fill each cap fully. I'll then return the stuffed mushrooms to the oven and bake for an additional 10 minutes until the mushrooms are tender and the filling is warmed through.
5. Serve: I'll plate the stuffed mushrooms and serve them immediately, garnishing with fresh herbs like parsley or basil if desired.

Nutritional Information (Per Serving):

- Calories: 280 | Protein: 10g | Fiber: 6g | Healthy Fats: 10g | Carbs: 32g

Tips:

1. If Portobello mushrooms aren't available, large cremini mushrooms can be used as a substitute.
2. Additional Flavor: For a burst of flavor, I like to drizzle a little balsamic glaze over the top before serving.
3. These stuffed mushrooms can be stored in the refrigerator for up to 2 days and reheated in the oven or microwave.

Cauliflower Steaks with Chimichurri Sauce

Gluten-Free, Dairy-Free, Soy-Free, Nut-Free

This Cauliflower Steaks with Chimichurri Sauce recipe is a delicious and nutrient-dense dinner option that aligns perfectly with the Good Energy principles. The dish features roasted cauliflower steaks topped with a vibrant chimichurri sauce, providing a balance of flavors and nutrients that support metabolic health and sustained energy.

Prep time: 15 minutes | Cooking time: 25 minutes | Servings: 2

Ingredients:

- For the Cauliflower Steaks:
- 1 large head of cauliflower, cut into 1-inch thick steaks
- 2 tbsp olive oil
- 1 tsp smoked paprika
- 1/2 tsp garlic powder
- Salt and pepper to taste
- For the Chimichurri Sauce:

- 1/2 cup fresh parsley, finely chopped
- 1/4 cup fresh cilantro, finely chopped
- 2 cloves garlic, minced
- 1/4 cup olive oil
- 2 tbsp red wine vinegar
- 1 tsp dried oregano
- 1/2 tsp red pepper flakes (optional for spice)
- Salt and pepper to taste

Step-by-Step Directions:

1. Prepare the Cauliflower Steaks: I'll begin by preheating the oven to 400°F (200°C). While the oven heats up, I'll remove the outer leaves of the cauliflower and trim the stem slightly, ensuring that the head stays intact. Next, I'll cut the cauliflower into 1-inch thick steaks, typically yielding 2-3 steaks per head, depending on its size. I'll brush each side of the cauliflower steaks with olive oil, then season them with smoked paprika, garlic powder, salt, and pepper.
2. Roast the Cauliflower: I'll place the seasoned cauliflower steaks on a baking sheet lined with parchment paper. I'll then roast them in the preheated oven for about 20-25 minutes, flipping halfway through, until they're golden brown and tender.
3. Prepare the Chimichurri Sauce: While the cauliflower is roasting, I'll make the chimichurri sauce. In a small bowl, I'll combine the chopped parsley, cilantro, and minced garlic. I'll add the olive oil, red wine vinegar, dried oregano, and red pepper flakes to the herbs, stirring everything together until well combined. I'll season the sauce with salt and pepper to taste.
4. Serve: Once the cauliflower steaks are roasted to perfection, I'll plate them and generously spoon the chimichurri sauce over each steak. I'll serve the cauliflower steaks immediately, garnishing with extra herbs if desired.

Nutritional Information (Per Serving):

- Calories: 220 | Protein: 4g | Fiber: 6g | Healthy Fats: 16g | Carbs: 15g

Tips:

1. Customizing the Spice Level: If you prefer a milder chimichurri, you can omit the red pepper flakes or reduce the amount used.
2. Storage: The chimichurri sauce can be made in advance and stored in the refrigerator for up to 3 days. The cauliflower steaks are best enjoyed fresh but can be reheated in the oven.

Serving Suggestions:

- These cauliflower steaks are versatile and pair well with a side of fresh mixed greens or a light avocado salad. For a heartier breakfast, you might consider adding a poached egg on top.

SNACKS AND APPETIZERS
Almond and Date Energy Balls
Gluten-Free, Dairy-Free, Soy-Free

These Almond and Date Energy Balls are a perfect snack or appetizer that provides a quick energy boost while aligning with the Good Energy principles. They are packed with natural sugars from the dates, healthy fats from the almonds, and a touch of fiber, making them a balanced snack option that supports metabolic health and provides sustained energy. The ingredients are simple, anti-inflammatory, and nutrient-dense, making these energy balls a go-to for a nutritious, satisfying snack.

Prep time: 10 minutes | Servings: 12 energy balls

Ingredients:

- 1 cup raw almonds
- 1 cup Medjool dates, pitted
- 2 tablespoons unsweetened shredded coconut (optional for rolling)
- 1 tablespoon chia seeds
- 1 tablespoon flaxseeds
- 1/2 teaspoon vanilla extract
- 1/4 teaspoon sea salt

Step-by-Step Directions:

1. Prepare the Ingredients: I start by making sure the dates are soft and moist. If they're a bit dry, I soak them in warm water for about 10 minutes, then drain them well before using.
2. Process the Almonds: In a food processor, I pulse the raw almonds until they're finely chopped, but not yet a powder. I want a bit of texture in these energy balls, so I don't over-process.
3. Add the Dates and Other Ingredients: I add the pitted dates, chia seeds, flaxseeds, vanilla extract, and sea salt to the food processor with the chopped almonds. I process everything together until the mixture comes together and is sticky enough to hold its shape when pressed. If the mixture is too dry, I add a small amount of water (about 1 teaspoon at a time) until the desired consistency is achieved.
4. Form the Energy Balls: Using my hands, I scoop out about a tablespoon of the mixture and roll it into a ball. If you like, you can roll each ball in shredded coconut for an extra touch of flavor and texture. I continue this process until all the mixture is used up, making about 12 energy balls.
5. Chill and Serve: I place the energy balls on a plate or in an airtight container and chill them in the refrigerator for at least 30 minutes before serving. This helps them firm up and makes them easier to handle.

Nutritional Information (Per Energy Ball):

- Calories: 90 | Protein: 2g | Fiber: 3g | Healthy Fats: 5g | Carbs: 10g

Tips:

1. Storage: These energy balls can be stored in an airtight container in the refrigerator for up to a week or in the freezer for up to a month, making them a convenient grab-and-go snack.
2. Customize: Feel free to add in other superfoods like cacao nibs, hemp seeds, or a dash of cinnamon to enhance the flavor and nutrient profile.

Serving Suggestions:

- These Almond and Date Energy Balls are perfect as a quick snack before a workout, a mid-afternoon pick-me-up, or even as a healthy dessert. They're portable, easy to make, and provide a balanced combination of nutrients to keep you energized throughout the day.

Cucumber and Carrot Sticks with Spicy Tahini Dip

Gluten-Free, Dairy-Free, Soy-Free, Nut-Free

This Cucumber and Carrot Sticks with Spicy Tahini Dip is a simple, refreshing snack or appetizer that aligns perfectly with the Good Energy principles. The crisp cucumber and carrot sticks are paired with a creamy, spicy tahini dip, providing a balance of healthy fats, fiber, and anti-inflammatory ingredients. This snack is light yet satisfying, making it a great option for maintaining energy levels and supporting metabolic health throughout the day.

Prep time: 15 minutes | Servings: 4

Ingredients:

- For the Cucumber and Carrot Sticks:
- 2 large cucumbers, sliced into sticks
- 4 large carrots, peeled and sliced into sticks
- For the Spicy Tahini Dip:
- 1/4 cup tahini
- 2 tablespoons fresh lemon juice
- 1 tablespoon extra-virgin olive oil
- 1 clove garlic, minced
- 1 tablespoon water (more as needed for consistency)
- 1/2 teaspoon ground cumin
- 1/4 teaspoon smoked paprika
- 1/4 teaspoon cayenne pepper (adjust to taste)
- 1/2 teaspoon sea salt
- 1/4 teaspoon black pepper
- 1 tablespoon fresh parsley, chopped (for garnish)

Step-by-Step Directions:

1. Prepare the Vegetables: I start by slicing the cucumbers and carrots into sticks. I aim for uniform sizes so they're easy to dip and eat. Once sliced, I arrange them on a serving platter.
2. Make the Spicy Tahini Dip: In a medium mixing bowl, I whisk together the tahini, fresh lemon juice, olive oil, minced garlic, and water. I add the ground cumin, smoked paprika, cayenne pepper, sea salt, and black pepper. I continue whisking until the mixture is smooth and creamy. If the dip is too thick, I add a little more water, one teaspoon at a time, until I reach the desired consistency.
3. Serve and Enjoy: I pour the spicy tahini dip into a serving bowl and garnish with freshly chopped parsley. I place the bowl in the center of the platter with the cucumber and carrot sticks. This snack is best enjoyed fresh, with the crisp vegetables perfectly complementing the creamy, flavorful dip.

Nutritional Information (Per Serving):

- Calories: 130 | Protein: 3g | Fiber: 4g | Healthy Fats: 10g | Carbs: 10g

Tips:

1. Adjust the Spice: If you prefer a milder dip, you can reduce or omit the cayenne pepper. For more heat, feel free to add extra.
2. Make It Ahead: The spicy tahini dip can be made ahead of time and stored in the refrigerator for up to 3 days. Just give it a good stir before serving.

Serving Suggestions:

- This Cucumber and Carrot Sticks with Spicy Tahini Dip is perfect as a quick snack, a light appetizer before dinner, or even as part of a larger spread for entertaining. Pair it with other fresh vegetables or gluten-free crackers for a variety of dipping options.

Roasted Garlic and Avocado Hummus

Gluten-Free, Dairy-Free, Soy-Free, Nut-Free

This Roasted Garlic and Avocado Hummus is a creamy, flavorful dip that perfectly aligns with the Good Energy principles. Combining the rich, buttery texture of avocado with the classic base of chickpeas and a hint of roasted garlic, this hummus is both satisfying and packed with healthy fats, fiber, and anti-inflammatory ingredients. It's a great snack or appetizer that supports metabolic health and provides a steady source of energy.

Prep time: 10 minutes | Cooking time: 30 minutes (for roasting garlic) | Servings: 6

Ingredients:

- For the Roasted Garlic:
- 1 head of garlic
- 1 tablespoon extra-virgin olive oil
- Pinch of sea salt
- For the Hummus:
- 1 can (15 ounces) chickpeas, drained and rinsed
- 1 ripe avocado
- Juice of 1 lemon (about 2 tablespoons)

- 2 tablespoons tahini
- 2 tablespoons extra-virgin olive oil
- 1/2 teaspoon ground cumin
- Sea salt and black pepper, to taste
- 2-3 tablespoons water (as needed for consistency)
- Fresh cilantro or parsley, for garnish (optional)

Step-by-Step Directions:

1. Roast the Garlic: First, I preheat the oven to 400°F (200°C). I slice off the top of the garlic head to expose the cloves, then drizzle it with olive oil and sprinkle with a pinch of sea salt. I wrap the garlic in foil and roast it in the oven for about 30 minutes, or until the cloves are soft and golden brown. Once roasted, I allow the garlic to cool before squeezing out the soft cloves.
2. Prepare the Hummus: In a food processor, I combine the drained chickpeas, roasted garlic cloves, ripe avocado, lemon juice, tahini, and cumin. I then add the extra-virgin olive oil, sea salt, and black pepper. I process everything together until smooth and creamy. If the hummus is too thick, I add water, one tablespoon at a time, until I reach the desired consistency.
3. Serve and Enjoy: I spoon the hummus into a serving bowl and, if desired, garnish it with fresh cilantro or parsley. This hummus pairs beautifully with fresh vegetable sticks, gluten-free crackers, or even as a spread for wraps and sandwiches.

Nutritional Information (Per Serving):

- Calories: 180 | Protein: 4g | Fiber: 6g | Healthy Fats: 13g | Carbs: 15g

Tips:

1. Storage: This hummus can be stored in an airtight container in the refrigerator for up to 3 days. The avocado may cause slight browning, but a quick stir will bring it back to its creamy green color.
2. Add Extra Flavor: For a bit of spice, you can add a pinch of cayenne pepper or smoked paprika to the hummus before blending.

Serving Suggestions:

- This Roasted Garlic and Avocado Hummus is a versatile snack that can be enjoyed in many ways. Serve it with fresh vegetable sticks like cucumbers, carrots, and bell peppers, or pair it with gluten-free pita chips or crackers. It's also delicious as a spread on sandwiches or wraps for a healthy, flavorful boost.

Cauliflower and Carrot Mash

Gluten-Free, Dairy-Free, Soy-Free, Nut-Free

This Cauliflower and Carrot Mash is a creamy, nutritious snack or appetizer that aligns perfectly with the Good Energy principles. The combination of cauliflower and carrots creates a light yet satisfying mash that's rich in fiber, vitamins, and antioxidants. It's an excellent low-carb alternative to traditional mashed potatoes, supporting metabolic health and providing anti-inflammatory benefits. This dish is both delicious and nourishing, making it a perfect addition to your Good Energy recipe collection.

Prep time: 10 minutes | Cooking time: 20 minutes | Servings: 4

Ingredients:

- 1 medium head of cauliflower, cut into florets
- 3 large carrots, peeled and chopped
- 2 tablespoons extra-virgin olive oil
- 2 cloves garlic, minced
- 1/2 teaspoon sea salt
- 1/4 teaspoon black pepper
- 1/2 teaspoon ground cumin (optional, for added flavor)
- Fresh parsley, chopped (for garnish, optional)

Step-by-Step Directions:

1. Steam the Vegetables: I begin by steaming the cauliflower florets and chopped carrots in a large pot with a steamer basket over boiling water. I cover and steam them for about 15 minutes, or until both the cauliflower and carrots are tender when pierced with a fork.
2. Sauté the Garlic: While the vegetables are steaming, I heat the extra-virgin olive oil in a small skillet over medium heat. I add the minced garlic and sauté for about 1-2 minutes until it becomes fragrant but not browned. This will infuse the oil with a rich garlic flavor that will enhance the mash.
3. Mash the Vegetables: Once the cauliflower and carrots are tender, I transfer them to a large mixing bowl or food processor. I add the sautéed garlic along with the olive oil, sea salt, black pepper, and ground cumin (if using). I then mash the mixture with a potato masher or blend it in the food processor until smooth and creamy. If you prefer a chunkier texture, you can mash them by hand.
4. Serve and Enjoy: I spoon the cauliflower and carrot mash into a serving bowl, garnishing with fresh chopped parsley if desired. This mash can be served warm as a side dish, snack, or appetizer.

Nutritional Information (Per Serving):

- Calories: 110 | Protein: 2g | Fiber: 5g | Healthy Fats: 7g | Carbs: 12g

Tips:

1. Customize the Flavor: You can add a pinch of nutmeg or smoked paprika to the mash for an extra layer of flavor.
2. Make It Creamier: For a creamier texture, you can add a tablespoon of coconut cream or unsweetened almond milk while mashing.

Serving Suggestions:

- This Cauliflower and Carrot Mash is a versatile dish that can be enjoyed in many ways. Serve it as a healthy snack, an appetizer alongside gluten-free crackers, or as a side dish to complement a protein-rich main course. It's also great as a base for roasted vegetables or a topping for shepherd's pie.

Roasted Red Pepper Hummus with Veggie Sticks

Gluten-Free, Dairy-Free, Soy-Free, Nut-Free

This Roasted Red Pepper Hummus with Veggie Sticks is a vibrant and flavorful snack that perfectly aligns with the Good Energy principles. The roasted red peppers add a sweet, smoky depth to the classic hummus base, creating a nutrient-rich dip that's packed with fiber, protein, and healthy fats. Paired with fresh veggie sticks, this snack is both satisfying and energizing, making it ideal for maintaining steady energy levels throughout the day.

Prep time: 15 minutes | Cooking time: 25 minutes (for roasting peppers) | Servings: 6

Ingredients:

- For the Roasted Red Pepper Hummus:
- 2 large red bell peppers
- 1 can (15 ounces) chickpeas, drained and rinsed
- 1/4 cup tahini
- 3 tablespoons fresh lemon juice
- 2 tablespoons extra-virgin olive oil
- 2 cloves garlic, minced
- 1/2 teaspoon ground cumin
- 1/2 teaspoon smoked paprika
- 1/2 teaspoon sea salt
- 1/4 teaspoon black pepper
- 2-3 tablespoons water (as needed for consistency)
- For the Veggie Sticks:
- 2 large carrots, peeled and cut into sticks
- 2 large cucumbers, sliced into sticks
- 2 bell peppers (any color), sliced into sticks
- 1 cup cherry tomatoes

Step-by-Step Directions:

1. Roast the Red Peppers: I start by preheating my oven to 400°F (200°C). I place the whole red bell peppers on a baking sheet and roast them in the oven for about 20-25 minutes, turning occasionally, until the skins are charred and the peppers are soft. Once roasted, I transfer the peppers to a bowl and cover them with a plate or plastic wrap to steam for about 10 minutes. This makes it easier to peel off the skins. After steaming, I peel off the skins, remove the seeds, and set the roasted peppers aside.
2. Prepare the Hummus: In a food processor, I combine the drained chickpeas, roasted red peppers, tahini, fresh lemon juice, olive oil, minced garlic, ground cumin, smoked paprika, sea salt, and black pepper. I blend everything until smooth and creamy. If the hummus is too thick, I add water, one tablespoon at a time, until I reach the desired consistency.
3. Prepare the Veggie Sticks: While the hummus is blending, I cut the carrots, cucumbers, and bell peppers into sticks. I arrange these along with the cherry tomatoes on a serving platter.
4. Serve and Enjoy: I transfer the roasted red pepper hummus to a serving bowl and place it on the platter with the veggie sticks. This dish is best enjoyed fresh, with the crisp vegetables perfectly complementing the creamy, flavorful hummus.

Nutritional Information (Per Serving):

- Calories: 140 | Protein: 4g | Fiber: 6g | Healthy Fats: 8g | Carbs: 15g

Tips:

1. Make It Ahead: The roasted red pepper hummus can be made a day ahead and stored in the refrigerator. The flavors will deepen as it sits, making it even more delicious.
2. Extra Flavor: For a bit more spice, you can add a pinch of cayenne pepper or a dash of hot sauce to the hummus before blending.

Baked Sweet Potato Fries with Spicy Avocado Dip

Gluten-Free, Dairy-Free, Soy-Free, Nut-Free

These Baked Sweet Potato Fries with Spicy Avocado Dip are a delicious and nutrient-packed snack or appetizer that perfectly aligns with the Good Energy principles. Sweet potatoes are rich in vitamins, fiber, and antioxidants, making them a great choice for supporting metabolic health. The spicy avocado dip adds a creamy, flavorful kick, packed with healthy fats and anti-inflammatory ingredients. This combination is satisfying and energizing, making it a perfect choice for a light meal or a snack.

Prep time: 15 minutes | Cooking time: 25 minutes | Servings: 4

Ingredients:

- For the Sweet Potato Fries:
- 2 large sweet potatoes, peeled and cut into thin fries
- 2 tablespoons extra-virgin olive oil
- 1/2 teaspoon sea salt
- 1/2 teaspoon smoked paprika
- 1/4 teaspoon garlic powder
- 1/4 teaspoon black pepper
- For the Spicy Avocado Dip:

- 1 large ripe avocado
- 1 tablespoon fresh lime juice
- 1 clove garlic, minced
- 1/4 teaspoon cayenne pepper (adjust to taste)
- 1/4 teaspoon sea salt
- 2 tablespoons fresh cilantro, chopped (optional for garnish)
- 1-2 tablespoons water (if needed to adjust consistency)

Step-by-Step Directions:

1. Preheat the Oven: I start by preheating the oven to 425°F (220°C) and line a baking sheet with parchment paper.
2. Prepare the Sweet Potato Fries: I toss the sweet potato fries in a large bowl with the extra-virgin olive oil, sea salt, smoked paprika, garlic powder, and black pepper. Once evenly coated, I spread the fries out in a single layer on the prepared baking sheet, ensuring they have space to crisp up.
3. Bake the Fries: I bake the sweet potato fries in the preheated oven for 20-25 minutes, flipping them halfway through, until they are golden brown and crispy on the edges.
4. Prepare the Spicy Avocado Dip: While the fries are baking, I prepare the avocado dip. In a medium bowl, I mash the ripe avocado with fresh lime juice, minced garlic, cayenne pepper, and sea salt. If the dip is too thick, I add a little water, one tablespoon at a time, until I reach the desired creamy consistency. I can also garnish with fresh cilantro if desired.
5. Serve and Enjoy: Once the sweet potato fries are done, I remove them from the oven and let them cool slightly. I then serve the fries alongside the spicy avocado dip for a satisfying, nutritious snack or appetizer.

Nutritional Information (Per Serving):

- Calories: 220 | Protein: 2g | Fiber: 6g | Healthy Fats: 14g | Carbs: 24g

Tips:

1. Crispier Fries: For extra crispy fries, I make sure to pat the sweet potato sticks dry with a paper towel before tossing them with the oil and seasoning.
2. Add Variety: You can add a sprinkle of chili powder or a dash of cinnamon to the fries for a different flavor profile.

Cucumber and Dill Greek Yogurt Dip

Gluten-Free, Soy-Free, Nut-Free

This Cucumber and Dill Greek Yogurt Dip is a refreshing, creamy snack that aligns perfectly with the Good Energy principles. Combining the probiotics from Greek yogurt with the hydrating and anti-inflammatory properties of cucumber and dill, this dip is both light and nourishing. It's a great way to support your metabolic health while enjoying a flavorful snack that's perfect for dipping fresh veggies or serving as a light appetizer.

Prep time: 10 minutes | Cooking time: None | Servings: 6

Ingredients:

- 1 cup Greek yogurt (preferably full-fat for creaminess)
- 1/2 large cucumber, finely grated and drained
- 2 tablespoons fresh dill, finely chopped
- 1 clove garlic, minced
- 1 tablespoon fresh lemon juice
- 1/2 teaspoon sea salt
- 1/4 teaspoon black pepper
- 1 tablespoon extra-virgin olive oil (optional for drizzling)

Step-by-Step Directions:

1. Prepare the Cucumber: I start by grating the cucumber using a fine grater. To prevent the dip from becoming watery, I place the grated cucumber in a clean kitchen towel or cheesecloth and gently squeeze out the excess moisture.
2. Mix the Dip: In a medium mixing bowl, I combine the Greek yogurt, grated cucumber, chopped dill, minced garlic, fresh lemon juice, sea salt, and black pepper. I stir everything together until it's well combined and creamy.
3. Optional Drizzle: If desired, I drizzle a small amount of extra-virgin olive oil over the top of the dip for added richness and flavor.
4. Chill and Serve: I cover the bowl and refrigerate the dip for at least 15 minutes to allow the flavors to meld together. Before serving, I give it a quick stir and then transfer it to a serving bowl.

Nutritional Information (Per Serving):

- Calories: 60 | Protein: 4g | Fiber: 1g | Healthy Fats: 2g | Carbs: 5g

Tips:

1. Make It Ahead: This dip can be made a day in advance and stored in the refrigerator. The flavors will intensify as it sits, making it even more delicious.
2. Customize the Flavor: If you enjoy a little extra kick, consider adding a pinch of cayenne pepper or some finely chopped fresh mint for a different flavor twist.

Serving Suggestions:

- This Cucumber and Dill Greek Yogurt Dip pairs wonderfully with fresh vegetable sticks such as carrots, celery, bell peppers, and cherry tomatoes. It also makes a great spread for sandwiches or wraps, adding a cool, creamy contrast to other ingredients.

Almond Flour Crackers with Olive Tapenade

Gluten-Free, Dairy-Free, Soy-Free

These Almond Flour Crackers with Olive Tapenade are a crunchy, flavorful snack that aligns perfectly with the Good Energy principles. The almond flour provides a healthy, low-carb base rich in protein and healthy fats, while the olive tapenade offers a punch of savory flavor packed with anti-inflammatory properties. This combination makes for a satisfying, nutrient-dense snack that supports metabolic health and provides steady energy.

Prep time: 15 minutes | Cooking time: 15 minutes | Servings: 6

Ingredients:

- For the Almond Flour Crackers:
- 2 cups almond flour
- 1 tablespoon ground flaxseed
- 1/2 teaspoon sea salt
- 1/2 teaspoon garlic powder (optional for added flavor)
- 1 large egg
- 1 tablespoon extra-virgin olive oil

- For the Olive Tapenade:
- 1 cup pitted Kalamata olives
- 1 tablespoon capers
- 1 clove garlic, minced
- 1 tablespoon fresh lemon juice
- 2 tablespoons extra-virgin olive oil
- 1/4 teaspoon dried oregano
- 1/4 teaspoon black pepper

Step-by-Step Directions:

1. Prepare the Almond Flour Crackers:
2. First, I preheat the oven to 350°F (175°C) and line a baking sheet with parchment paper. In a mixing bowl, I combine the almond flour, ground flaxseed, sea salt, and garlic powder. I then add the egg and olive oil, mixing until a dough forms.
3. Roll Out the Dough: I place the dough between two sheets of parchment paper and roll it out to about 1/8-inch thickness. I carefully remove the top sheet of parchment and cut the dough into small squares using a pizza cutter or a sharp knife. Once cut, I transfer the entire sheet of parchment with the dough onto the baking sheet.
4. Bake the Crackers: I bake the crackers in the preheated oven for 12-15 minutes, or until they are golden brown and crispy. After baking, I let them cool completely on the baking sheet to allow them to crisp up further.
5. Prepare the Olive Tapenade: While the crackers are baking, I make the olive tapenade. In a food processor, I combine the pitted olives, capers, minced garlic, lemon juice, olive oil, dried oregano, and black pepper. I pulse the mixture until it is finely chopped but still has some texture. If the tapenade is too thick, I add a bit more olive oil to reach the desired consistency.
6. Serve and Enjoy: Once the crackers have cooled, I serve them with the olive tapenade on the side. The combination of the crunchy crackers and the rich, savory tapenade makes for a perfect snack or appetizer.

Nutritional Information (Per Serving):

- Calories: 210 | Protein: 6g | Fiber: 4g | Healthy Fats: 18g | Carbs: 8g

Tips:

1. Storage: The almond flour crackers can be stored in an airtight container at room temperature for up to a week. The olive tapenade can be refrigerated in a sealed container for up to 5 days.
2. Flavor Variations: You can add different herbs or spices to the cracker dough, such as rosemary or smoked paprika, to create a variety of flavors.

Baked Kale Chips with Sea Salt

Gluten-Free, Dairy-Free, Soy-Free, Nut-Free

These Baked Kale Chips with Sea Salt are a crunchy, savory snack that fits perfectly into the Good Energy principles. Kale is a powerhouse of nutrients, packed with vitamins, fiber, and antioxidants that support metabolic health and reduce inflammation. These chips are a simple, healthy alternative to store-bought snacks, offering a satisfying crunch with minimal ingredients and maximum nutrition.

Prep time: 10 minutes | Cooking time: 15 minutes | Servings: 4

Ingredients:

- 1 large bunch of kale (curly or lacinato)
- 1 tablespoon extra-virgin olive oil
- 1/2 teaspoon sea salt
- 1/4 teaspoon garlic powder (optional for added flavor)

Step-by-Step Directions:

1. Preheat the Oven: I begin by preheating the oven to 300°F (150°C). This lower temperature helps to bake the kale evenly and prevents burning.
2. Prepare the Kale: First, I wash the kale thoroughly and then dry it completely using a salad spinner or clean kitchen towels. Any remaining moisture can make the chips soggy. Once dry, I remove the tough stems and tear the kale into bite-sized pieces.
3. Season the Kale: I place the kale pieces in a large mixing bowl and drizzle them with the extra-virgin olive oil. I then sprinkle the sea salt and garlic powder (if using) over the kale. Using my hands, I massage the oil and seasoning into the kale, ensuring each piece is evenly coated.
4. Bake the Kale Chips: I spread the kale pieces in a single layer on a large baking sheet, making sure they don't overlap. This helps them to crisp up nicely. I bake the kale in the preheated oven for 12-15 minutes, checking after 10 minutes to ensure they don't burn. The chips are ready when they are crispy and slightly browned on the edges.
5. Cool and Serve: Once baked, I remove the kale chips from the oven and let them cool on the baking sheet for a few minutes. They will continue to crisp up as they cool. I then transfer the chips to a serving bowl and enjoy immediately.

Nutritional Information (Per Serving):

- Calories: 70 | Protein: 2g | Fiber: 2g | Healthy Fats: 4g | Carbs: 7g

Tips:

1. Storage: If you have leftovers, store the kale chips in an airtight container at room temperature. They are best enjoyed fresh but will keep for 1-2 days.
2. Flavor Variations: You can add other seasonings like smoked paprika, nutritional yeast for a cheesy flavor, or chili powder for a spicy kick.

Serving Suggestions:

- These Baked Kale Chips with Sea Salt are perfect for a quick snack or as a crunchy side to your lunch. They also make a great appetizer for parties or gatherings, offering a healthy alternative to traditional chips. Pair them with your favorite dip or enjoy them on their own.

Deviled Eggs with Avocado and Paprika

Gluten-Free, Dairy-Free, Soy-Free, Nut-Free

These Deviled Eggs with Avocado and Paprika are a creamy, flavorful snack that perfectly aligns with the Good Energy principles. By replacing traditional mayonnaise with heart-healthy avocado, you get a nutrient-dense filling that's rich in healthy fats, vitamins, and antioxidants. The addition of paprika not only enhances the flavor but also adds a subtle smokiness that pairs well with the creamy texture. This snack is perfect for supporting metabolic health and providing a satisfying, energy-boosting treat.

Prep time: 15 minutes | Cooking time: 10 minutes (for boiling eggs) | Servings: 6 (12 deviled eggs)

Ingredients:

- 6 large eggs
- 1 ripe avocado
- 1 tablespoon fresh lemon juice
- 1 teaspoon Dijon mustard
- 1/2 teaspoon sea salt
- 1/4 teaspoon black pepper
- 1/4 teaspoon smoked paprika, plus more for garnish
- Fresh chives, chopped (optional for garnish)

Step-by-Step Directions:

1. Boil the Eggs: I start by placing the eggs in a medium-sized saucepan and covering them with cold water. I bring the water to a boil over medium-high heat. Once boiling, I cover the pot, remove it from the heat, and let the eggs sit for 10 minutes.
2. Prepare the Avocado Filling: While the eggs are cooking, I cut the ripe avocado in half, remove the pit, and scoop the flesh into a medium mixing bowl. I add the fresh lemon juice, Dijon mustard, sea salt, black pepper, and smoked paprika to the avocado. Using a fork or potato masher, I mash everything together until smooth and well combined.
3. Peel and Halve the Eggs: After the eggs have finished cooking, I drain the hot water and run cold water over the eggs to cool them down quickly. Once cooled, I gently peel the eggs and slice them in half lengthwise. I carefully remove the yolks and add them to the avocado mixture, mashing them together until smooth.
4. Fill the Egg Whites: Using a spoon or a piping bag, I fill each egg white half with the avocado-yolk mixture. I like to slightly overfill each egg for a generous serving.
5. Garnish and Serve: I sprinkle a little extra smoked paprika over the top of the filled eggs for garnish. If desired, I also add a sprinkle of chopped fresh chives for added flavor and color. The eggs are now ready to serve!

Nutritional Information (Per Serving):

- Calories: 120 | Protein: 6g | Fiber: 2g | Healthy Fats: 9g | Carbs: 2g

Tips:

1. Make Ahead: These deviled eggs can be made a few hours in advance and stored in the refrigerator. Just cover them tightly to prevent the avocado from browning.
2. Spice it Up: If you like a bit of heat, you can add a dash of hot sauce or a pinch of cayenne pepper to the avocado mixture.

Spicy Roasted Chickpeas

Gluten-Free, Dairy-Free, Soy-Free, Nut-Free

Spicy Roasted Chickpeas are a crunchy and satisfying snack that perfectly aligns with the Good Energy principles. These chickpeas are seasoned with a blend of spices that not only add flavor but also contribute to your metabolic health. They are an excellent source of plant-based protein, fiber, and healthy fats, making them a great snack to keep you energized throughout the day.

Prep time: 10 minutes | Cooking time: 30 minutes | Servings: 4

Ingredients:

- 1 can (15 oz) chickpeas, drained and rinsed
- 1 tbsp olive oil
- 1 tsp smoked paprika
- 1/2 tsp ground cumin
- 1/2 tsp garlic powder
- 1/4 tsp cayenne pepper (adjust to taste)
- 1/2 tsp sea salt
- 1/4 tsp black pepper

Step-by-Step Directions:

1. Preheat the Oven: I'll start by preheating the oven to 400°F (200°C). While the oven is heating, I'll prepare the chickpeas.
2. Prepare the Chickpeas: After draining and rinsing the chickpeas, I'll spread them out on a clean kitchen towel or paper towel to dry them thoroughly. Removing excess moisture is crucial for achieving a crispy texture.
3. Season the Chickpeas: In a mixing bowl, I'll toss the dried chickpeas with olive oil, ensuring they're evenly coated. Then, I'll add the smoked paprika, ground cumin, garlic powder, cayenne pepper, sea salt, and black pepper, stirring well to coat the chickpeas with the spices.
4. Roast the Chickpeas: I'll spread the seasoned chickpeas in a single layer on a baking sheet lined with parchment paper. I'll roast them in the preheated oven for 25-30 minutes, shaking the pan halfway through to ensure even roasting. The chickpeas should be golden and crispy.
5. Cool and Serve: Once roasted, I'll remove the chickpeas from the oven and allow them to cool for a few minutes. They'll continue to crisp up as they cool.

Nutritional Information (Per Serving):

- Calories: 120 | Protein: 5g | Fiber: 5g | Healthy Fats: 3g | Carbs: 18g

Tips:

1. Storage: Store the roasted chickpeas in an airtight container at room temperature for up to 4 days. They're best enjoyed fresh for maximum crunch.
2. Adjusting Spice: Feel free to adjust the cayenne pepper if you prefer a milder or spicier snack. You can also experiment with other spices like turmeric or chili powder.

Serving Suggestions:

- These Spicy Roasted Chickpeas are a versatile snack. You can enjoy them on their own, sprinkle them over salads for extra crunch, or even mix them into a trail mix with dried fruits and seeds. They're also great as a topping for soups to add a bit of texture and spice.

Zucchini Chips with Garlic Dip

Gluten-Free, Dairy-Free, Soy-Free, Nut-Free

Zucchini Chips with Garlic Dip are a light, crunchy snack that fits perfectly into the Good Energy lifestyle. These chips are baked, not fried, keeping them low in unhealthy fats while providing a satisfying crunch. Paired with a creamy garlic dip, this snack offers a burst of flavor while keeping things healthy and balanced.

Prep time: 15 minutes | Cooking time: 1 hour | Servings: 4

Ingredients:

- For the Zucchini Chips:
- 2 medium zucchinis, thinly sliced
- 1 tbsp olive oil
- 1/2 tsp sea salt
- 1/4 tsp black pepper
- 1/4 tsp garlic powder (optional)
- For the Garlic Dip:

- 1/2 cup coconut yogurt (or any dairy-free yogurt)
- 1 garlic clove, minced
- 1 tbsp lemon juice
- 1 tbsp fresh dill, chopped
- 1/4 tsp sea salt
- 1/4 tsp black pepper

Step-by-Step Directions:

1. Preheat the Oven: I'll begin by preheating the oven to 225°F (110°C). While the oven heats up, I'll prepare the zucchini.
2. Prepare the Zucchini Chips: Using a mandoline or a sharp knife, I'll slice the zucchinis into very thin rounds, about 1/8 inch thick. The thinner the slices, the crispier the chips will be. In a mixing bowl, I'll toss the zucchini slices with olive oil, sea salt, black pepper, and garlic powder until they are evenly coated.
3. Bake the Zucchini Chips: I'll lay the zucchini slices out in a single layer on a baking sheet lined with parchment paper, making sure they don't overlap. I'll bake the zucchini in the preheated oven for about 1 to 1.5 hours, or until the chips are crispy and golden. I'll check them periodically to ensure they don't burn, flipping them halfway through baking.
4. Prepare the Garlic Dip: While the zucchini chips are baking, I'll make the garlic dip. In a small bowl, I'll combine the coconut yogurt, minced garlic, lemon juice, fresh dill, sea salt, and black pepper. I'll mix everything together until smooth and well-combined. I'll then refrigerate the dip until the chips are ready to serve.
5. Serve: Once the zucchini chips are done baking, I'll let them cool for a few minutes to crisp up even more. Then, I'll serve them with the garlic dip on the side for dipping.

Nutritional Information (Per Serving):

- Calories: 80 | Protein: 2g | Fiber: 2g | Healthy Fats: 4g | Carbs: 9g

Tips:

1. Slice Evenly: Make sure the zucchini slices are as even as possible for uniform baking.
2. Storage: Store any leftover chips in an airtight container at room temperature for up to 2 days, although they're best enjoyed fresh.

Serving Suggestions:

- These Zucchini Chips with Garlic Dip make a great snack on their own, or they can be served as a side dish with sandwiches or wraps. You can also pair them with other dips like guacamole or hummus for variety.

Avocado and Tomato Salsa with Plantain Chips

Gluten-Free, Dairy-Free, Soy-Free, Nut-Free

Avocado and Tomato Salsa with Plantain Chips is a vibrant, fresh appetizer that fits seamlessly into the Good Energy lifestyle. The creamy avocado combined with juicy tomatoes and zesty lime makes for a refreshing salsa, while the baked plantain chips offer a crunchy, satisfying base. This recipe is rich in healthy fats, fiber, and essential nutrients, supporting metabolic health and providing sustained energy.

Prep time: 15 minutes | Cooking time: 20 minutes | Servings: 4

Ingredients:

- For the Plantain Chips:
- 2 large green plantains, peeled and thinly sliced
- 1 tbsp coconut oil, melted
- 1/2 tsp sea salt
- For the Avocado and Tomato Salsa:
- 2 ripe avocados, diced
- 1 cup cherry tomatoes, quartered
- 1/4 cup red onion, finely chopped
- 1/4 cup fresh cilantro, chopped
- Juice of 1 lime
- 1 garlic clove, minced
- 1/4 tsp sea salt
- 1/4 tsp black pepper

Step-by-Step Directions:

1. Preheat the Oven: I'll start by preheating the oven to 375°F (190°C). As the oven heats, I'll prepare the plantain chips.
2. Prepare the Plantain Chips: I'll slice the plantains as thinly as possible using a sharp knife or mandoline. The thinner the slices, the crispier the chips. In a large bowl, I'll toss the plantain slices with the melted coconut oil and sea salt until they're evenly coated. I'll arrange the plantain slices in a single layer on a baking sheet lined with parchment paper, making sure they don't overlap. I'll bake the plantains in the preheated oven for about 15-20 minutes, flipping them halfway through, until they're golden brown and crispy.
3. Prepare the Avocado and Tomato Salsa: While the plantain chips are baking, I'll prepare the salsa. In a medium bowl, I'll combine the diced avocados, cherry tomatoes, red onion, cilantro, lime juice, minced garlic, sea salt, and black pepper. I'll gently toss the ingredients together until they're well combined, being careful not to mash the avocado. Once mixed, I'll set the salsa aside.
4. Serve: Once the plantain chips are ready, I'll let them cool slightly before serving. I'll then serve the chips alongside the avocado and tomato salsa, perfect for dipping.

Nutritional Information (Per Serving):

- Calories: 210 | Protein: 3g | Fiber: 5g | Healthy Fats: 14g | Carbs: 20g

Tips:

1. Plantain Ripeness: Using green plantains is key to getting crispy chips. Ripe plantains are sweeter and softer, which won't work as well for chips.
2. Salsa Variations: For extra flavor, I can add diced jalapeños or a pinch of smoked paprika to the salsa.

Serving Suggestions:

- This dish is perfect as an appetizer or snack. It's also great for parties or as a side dish for a light meal. You can enjoy it with a variety of other dips or spreads to add more variety.

DESSERTS RECIPES
Coconut Chia Pudding with Mango
Gluten-Free, Dairy-Free, Soy-Free

This Coconut Chia Pudding with Mango is a refreshing and nutritious dessert that aligns perfectly with the Good Energy principles. Chia seeds are a fantastic source of omega-3 fatty acids, fiber, and antioxidants, all of which support metabolic health. Combined with the creamy richness of coconut milk and the natural sweetness of fresh mango, this dessert is not only satisfying but also packed with nutrients that help reduce inflammation and provide balanced energy.

Prep time: 10 minutes | Cooking time: 2 hours (or overnight) | Servings: 4

Ingredients:

- 1/4 cup chia seeds
- 1 cup coconut milk (full-fat for creaminess)
- 1/2 cup water
- 1 tablespoon maple syrup (optional, for sweetness)
- 1/2 teaspoon vanilla extract
- 1 large ripe mango, peeled and diced
- 2 tablespoons unsweetened shredded coconut (optional, for garnish)

Step-by-Step Directions:

1. Mix the Pudding Base: In a medium mixing bowl, I combine the chia seeds, coconut milk, water, maple syrup (if using), and vanilla extract. I whisk everything together until the mixture is well combined and the chia seeds are evenly distributed.
2. Let It Set: I cover the bowl and place it in the refrigerator to chill for at least 2 hours, or overnight if possible. During this time, the chia seeds will absorb the liquid and expand, creating a thick, pudding-like consistency.
3. Prepare the Mango: While the pudding is setting, I peel and dice the ripe mango into small, bite-sized pieces. I set it aside in the refrigerator until I'm ready to serve.
4. Assemble the Dessert: Once the chia pudding has thickened, I give it a good stir to ensure an even texture. I then spoon the pudding into individual serving bowls or glasses. I top each serving with a generous portion of the diced mango.
5. Garnish and Serve: For an added touch, I like to sprinkle a little unsweetened shredded coconut over the top of each serving. The pudding is now ready to enjoy!

Nutritional Information (Per Serving):

- Calories: 180 | Protein: 3g | Fiber: 7g | Healthy Fats: 12g | Carbs: 17g

Tips:

1. Make It Ahead: This chia pudding is a great make-ahead dessert. It keeps well in the refrigerator for up to 3 days, making it perfect for meal prepping.
2. Adjust Sweetness: Depending on the sweetness of the mango, you might want to adjust the amount of maple syrup or skip it altogether for a naturally sweet treat.

Coconut Macaroons with Dark Chocolate Drizzle

Gluten-Free, Dairy-Free, Soy-Free

These Coconut Macaroons with Dark Chocolate Drizzle are a delightful dessert that aligns perfectly with the Good Energy principles. Coconut provides healthy fats and fiber, supporting metabolic health, while dark chocolate offers antioxidants and anti-inflammatory benefits. This recipe is simple yet satisfying, offering a sweet treat that won't spike your blood sugar but will satisfy your sweet cravings.

Prep time: 10 minutes | Cooking time: 15 minutes | Servings: 12 macaroons

Ingredients:

- 2 1/2 cups unsweetened shredded coconut
- 1/2 cup almond flour
- 1/2 cup pure maple syrup
- 1/4 cup coconut oil, melted
- 1 teaspoon vanilla extract
- 1/4 teaspoon sea salt
- 1/2 cup dark chocolate chips (dairy-free, 70% cacao or higher)

Step-by-Step Directions:

1. Preheat the Oven: I start by preheating the oven to 350°F (175°C) and line a baking sheet with parchment paper to prevent sticking.
2. Mix the Ingredients: In a large mixing bowl, I combine the shredded coconut, almond flour, maple syrup, melted coconut oil, vanilla extract, and sea salt. I stir everything together until the mixture is well combined and holds together when pressed.
3. Shape the Macaroons: Using a tablespoon or a small cookie scoop, I scoop out the mixture and form it into small, compact mounds. I place each mound onto the prepared baking sheet, spacing them about 1 inch apart.
4. Bake the Macaroons: I bake the macaroons in the preheated oven for 12-15 minutes, or until they are golden brown on the edges. Once done, I remove them from the oven and let them cool completely on the baking sheet.
5. Prepare the Dark Chocolate Drizzle: While the macaroons are cooling, I melt the dark chocolate chips. I do this by placing the chocolate in a heatproof bowl and microwaving it in 20-second intervals, stirring after each, until fully melted and smooth.
6. Drizzle the Chocolate: Once the macaroons have cooled, I use a spoon to drizzle the melted dark chocolate over the top of each macaroon. I let the chocolate set at room temperature, or I place the macaroons in the refrigerator for faster setting.

Nutritional Information (Per Serving):

- Calories: 150 | Protein: 2g | Fiber: 3g | Healthy Fats: 12g | Carbs: 10g

Tips:

1. Storage: Store these macaroons in an airtight container at room temperature for up to 5 days or in the refrigerator for up to 1 week.
2. Variation: For a nut-free version, you can replace the almond flour with an equal amount of coconut flour.

Almond and Date Bars with Coconut Flakes

Gluten-Free, Dairy-Free, Soy-Free

These Almond and Date Bars with Coconut Flakes are a wholesome, naturally sweetened dessert that perfectly aligns with the Good Energy principles. The combination of almonds, dates, and coconut provides a balanced mix of healthy fats, fiber, and natural sugars, which helps sustain energy levels and supports metabolic health. These bars are easy to make and are perfect for a snack or a dessert that satisfies your sweet tooth while keeping you on track with your health goals.

Prep time: 15 minutes | Cooking time: None (chill time: 1 hour) | Servings: 12 bars

Ingredients:

- 1 1/2 cups raw almonds
- 1 cup Medjool dates, pitted
- 1/2 cup unsweetened shredded coconut, plus extra for topping
- 1/4 cup almond butter
- 1 tablespoon coconut oil, melted
- 1 teaspoon vanilla extract
- 1/4 teaspoon sea salt

Step-by-Step Directions:

1. Prepare the Almonds and Dates: I start by placing the raw almonds into a food processor and pulse until they are finely chopped. Then, I add the pitted Medjool dates to the processor and pulse again until the mixture is well combined and forms a sticky dough.
2. Add the Remaining Ingredients: Next, I add the shredded coconut, almond butter, melted coconut oil, vanilla extract, and sea salt to the food processor. I continue pulsing until all the ingredients are fully combined and the mixture begins to clump together.
3. Form the Bars: I line an 8x8 inch baking pan with parchment paper, leaving some overhang for easy removal. I then transfer the almond and date mixture into the pan. Using my hands or the back of a spoon, I press the mixture firmly and evenly into the pan to form a compact layer.
4. Chill the Bars: Once the mixture is evenly pressed, I sprinkle a bit of extra shredded coconut on top for added texture. I then place the pan in the refrigerator to chill for at least 1 hour, or until the bars are firm and set.
5. Cut and Serve: After chilling, I use the parchment paper to lift the block out of the pan. I cut it into 12 bars using a sharp knife. The bars are now ready to serve!

Nutritional Information (Per Serving):

- Calories: 180 | Protein: 4g | Fiber: 3g | Healthy Fats: 12g | Carbs: 15g

Tips:

1. Storage: These bars can be stored in an airtight container in the refrigerator for up to 1 week or in the freezer for up to 3 months.
2. Add-ins: You can customize these bars by adding ingredients like chia seeds, flaxseeds, or dark chocolate chips to the mixture for additional texture and flavor.

Serving Suggestions:

- These Almond and Date Bars with Coconut Flakes are perfect as a quick snack, a healthy dessert, or even a pre-workout energy boost. Pair them with a cup of herbal tea for a satisfying treat that's both delicious and nutritious.

Baked Pears with Cinnamon and Walnuts

Gluten-Free, Dairy-Free, Soy-Free

These Baked Pears with Cinnamon and Walnuts are a simple yet elegant dessert that perfectly aligns with the Good Energy principles. Pears are naturally sweet and rich in fiber, which supports healthy digestion and metabolic health. Combined with the anti-inflammatory benefits of cinnamon and the healthy fats from walnuts, this dessert is not only delicious but also nourishing, providing a warm and comforting treat without compromising on nutrition.

Prep time: 10 minutes | Cooking time: 25 minutes | Servings: 4

Ingredients:

- 2 large ripe pears
- 1/4 cup walnuts, chopped
- 1 tablespoon coconut oil, melted
- 1 teaspoon ground cinnamon
- 1 tablespoon maple syrup (optional, for added sweetness)
- 1/2 teaspoon vanilla extract

Step-by-Step Directions:

1. Preheat the Oven: I start by preheating the oven to 350°F (175°C). I line a baking dish with parchment paper or lightly grease it with coconut oil to prevent sticking.
2. Prepare the Pears: I wash the pears thoroughly, then cut them in half lengthwise. Using a spoon or melon baller, I scoop out the core and seeds, creating a small well in the center of each pear half.
3. Mix the Filling: In a small bowl, I combine the chopped walnuts, melted coconut oil, ground cinnamon, maple syrup (if using), and vanilla extract. I stir until the walnuts are evenly coated with the mixture.
4. Assemble the Pears: I place the pear halves in the prepared baking dish, cut side up. I spoon the walnut mixture into the wells of each pear half, dividing it evenly among them.
5. Bake the Pears: I bake the pears in the preheated oven for about 25 minutes, or until they are tender and slightly caramelized. The walnuts should be toasted, and the pears should be soft enough to pierce easily with a fork.
6. Serve: Once baked, I remove the pears from the oven and let them cool slightly before serving. These pears are best enjoyed warm, straight from the oven.

Nutritional Information (Per Serving):

- Calories: 180 | Protein: 2g | Fiber: 5g | Healthy Fats: 8g | Carbs: 26g

Tips:

1. Toppings: For added richness, you can drizzle a little extra maple syrup over the pears before serving or add a dollop of coconut yogurt or a scoop of dairy-free vanilla ice cream.
2. Make it Nut-Free: If you need a nut-free version, you can replace the walnuts with sunflower seeds or pumpkin seeds.

Serving Suggestions:

- These Baked Pears with Cinnamon and Walnuts make a perfect dessert for a cozy evening or a special occasion. They are also a great option for breakfast when served with a side of plain yogurt. The warm, spiced flavor of the pears pairs wonderfully with a cup of herbal tea or a decaf coffee.

Raw Cacao and Avocado Mousse

Gluten-Free, Dairy-Free, Soy-Free

This Raw Cacao and Avocado Mousse is a rich, velvety dessert that aligns beautifully with the Good Energy principles. Avocado provides a creamy base loaded with healthy fats and fiber, supporting heart health and stable blood sugar levels. Raw cacao is packed with antioxidants and magnesium, promoting relaxation and reducing inflammation. This dessert is indulgent yet healthy, offering a delicious way to satisfy your chocolate cravings while nourishing your body.

Prep time: 10 minutes | Servings: 4

Ingredients:

- 2 large ripe avocados
- 1/4 cup raw cacao powder
- 1/4 cup maple syrup (or to taste)
- 2 teaspoons vanilla extract
- 1/4 cup coconut milk (full-fat for creaminess)
- Pinch of sea salt
- Fresh berries, for garnish (optional)
- Shaved dark chocolate, for garnish (optional)

Step-by-Step Directions:

1. Prepare the Avocados: I start by cutting the avocados in half, removing the pits, and scooping the flesh into a high-speed blender or food processor.
2. Blend the Ingredients: Next, I add the raw cacao powder, maple syrup, vanilla extract, coconut milk, and a pinch of sea salt to the blender with the avocado. I blend everything on high until the mixture is smooth and creamy, stopping to scrape down the sides as needed.
3. Taste and Adjust: I give the mousse a taste and adjust the sweetness if necessary by adding a bit more maple syrup. If the mixture is too thick, I add a little more coconut milk, one tablespoon at a time, until it reaches the desired consistency.Chill the Mousse:
4. Once the mousse is smooth and well-blended, I transfer it into serving bowls or glasses. I cover them with plastic wrap and refrigerate for at least 30 minutes to allow the flavors to meld and the mousse to firm up slightly.
5. Garnish and Serve: Before serving, I like to top the mousse with fresh berries and shaved dark chocolate for an extra touch of flavor and texture. The mousse is now ready to enjoy!

Nutritional Information (Per Serving):

- Calories: 230 | Protein: 3g | Fiber: 7g | Healthy Fats: 18g | Carbs: 17g

Tips:

1. Make Ahead: This mousse can be made ahead of time and stored in the refrigerator for up to 2 days. Just be sure to cover it tightly to prevent the avocado from browning.
2. Optional Add-ins: For a deeper chocolate flavor, I sometimes add a tablespoon of espresso powder or a pinch of cinnamon to the mix.

Serving Suggestions:

- This Raw Cacao and Avocado Mousse is perfect for a decadent yet healthy dessert. It's a great choice for dinner parties or special occasions when you want to impress guests with a treat that's both delicious and nutritious. Pair it with a glass of almond milk or herbal tea for a complete dessert experience.

Raspberry Chia Seed Jam Tart

Gluten-Free, Dairy-Free, Soy-Free

This Raspberry Chia Seed Jam Tart is a delightful dessert that beautifully aligns with the Good Energy principles. The tart features a nutrient-rich almond flour crust and is filled with a naturally sweetened raspberry chia jam. Chia seeds provide omega-3 fatty acids and fiber, supporting heart health and stable blood sugar levels, while raspberries are loaded with antioxidants and vitamins. This tart is not only delicious but also nourishing, offering a perfect balance of flavors and nutrients that support overall well-being.

Prep time: 20 minutes | Cooking time: 15 minutes | Chill time: 1 hour | Servings: 8

Ingredients:

- For the Crust:
- 1 1/2 cups almond flour
- 1/4 cup coconut oil, melted
- 2 tablespoons maple syrup
- 1/4 teaspoon sea salt
- 1/2 teaspoon vanilla extract

- For the Raspberry Chia Seed Jam:
- 2 cups fresh or frozen raspberries
- 2 tablespoons chia seeds
- 2 tablespoons maple syrup
- 1/2 teaspoon vanilla extract

Step-by-Step Directions:

1. Prepare the Crust: Mix the Ingredients: I start by preheating the oven to 350°F (175°C) and lining a tart pan with parchment paper. In a medium mixing bowl, I combine the almond flour, melted coconut oil, maple syrup, sea salt, and vanilla extract. I stir until the mixture forms a dough-like consistency.
2. Press into the Pan: I press the dough evenly into the bottom and up the sides of the prepared tart pan to form a crust. I make sure it's firmly packed to avoid crumbling.
3. Bake the Crust: I place the crust in the preheated oven and bake for about 10-12 minutes, or until it's golden brown. Once baked, I set it aside to cool while I prepare the filling.
4. Make the Raspberry Chia Seed Jam: Cook the Raspberries: In a small saucepan, I heat the raspberries over medium heat until they begin to break down and release their juices, about 5 minutes.
5. Add the Chia Seeds: I remove the saucepan from the heat and stir in the chia seeds, maple syrup, and vanilla extract. I let the mixture sit for 5-10 minutes, allowing the chia seeds to thicken the jam.
6. Assemble the Tart: Fill the Crust: Once the crust is completely cooled, I spoon the raspberry chia seed jam into the tart shell, spreading it out evenly with the back of a spoon.
7. Chill the Tart: I place the tart in the refrigerator to chill for at least 1 hour, allowing the jam to set and the flavors to meld.
8. Serve: Garnish (Optional): Before serving, I sometimes garnish the tart with a few fresh raspberries or a sprinkle of shredded coconut for added texture and flavor. The tart is best served cold, straight from the refrigerator.

Nutritional Information (Per Serving):

- Calories: 200 | Protein: 4g | Fiber: 5g | Healthy Fats: 14g | Carbs: 16g

Tips:

1. Storage: Store the tart in an airtight container in the refrigerator for up to 5 days.
2. Variation: You can substitute the raspberries with other berries, such as strawberries or blueberries, to change the flavor profile.

Lemon-Coconut Energy Balls

Gluten-Free, Dairy-Free, Soy-Free

These Lemon-Coconut Energy Balls are a zesty and refreshing treat that perfectly aligns with the Good Energy principles. Packed with healthy fats, fiber, and antioxidants, these energy balls support metabolic health and provide a quick, nutrient-dense snack that can help sustain your energy throughout the day. The combination of lemon and coconut gives these bites a bright and tropical flavor, making them both satisfying and revitalizing.

Prep time: 15 minutes | Cooking time: 15 minutes | Servings: 12 energy balls

Ingredients:

- 1 cup almond flour
- 1/2 cup unsweetened shredded coconut, plus extra for rolling
- 2 tablespoons coconut oil, melted
- 2 tablespoons maple syrup
- Zest of 1 large lemon
- Juice of 1 large lemon
- 1/2 teaspoon vanilla extract
- Pinch of sea salt

Step-by-Step Directions:

1. Mix the Ingredients: I start by adding the almond flour, shredded coconut, melted coconut oil, maple syrup, lemon zest, lemon juice, vanilla extract, and a pinch of sea salt into a large mixing bowl. Using a spoon or spatula, I mix everything together until a dough forms. The mixture should be sticky enough to hold together when pressed.
2. Form the Balls: I scoop out about 1 tablespoon of the mixture at a time and roll it between my palms to form a ball. I continue this process until all the dough is used, making approximately 12 energy balls.
3. Roll in Coconut (Optional): For an extra touch of flavor and texture, I like to roll the energy balls in some additional shredded coconut, pressing lightly so that the coconut adheres to the surface.
4. Chill the Energy Balls: Once all the balls are formed, I place them on a plate or in a container and refrigerate them for at least 30 minutes. Chilling helps to firm them up and enhance their flavor.
5. Serve: After chilling, the energy balls are ready to enjoy. They can be stored in an airtight container in the refrigerator for up to a week.

Nutritional Information (Per Serving):

- Calories: 90 | Protein: 2g | Fiber: 2g | Healthy Fats: 7g | Carbs: 5g

Tips:

1. Make it Nut-Free: If you need a nut-free version, you can replace the almond flour with oat flour or sunflower seed flour.
2. Adjusting Sweetness: Depending on your preference, you can adjust the sweetness by adding a little more or less maple syrup.

Serving Suggestions:

- These Lemon-Coconut Energy Balls make an ideal snack or a quick dessert. They're perfect for a post-workout treat or a midday energy boost. Pair them with a cup of green tea or a refreshing glass of lemon water to complement their bright, citrusy flavor.

Spiced Apple and Almond Crisp

Gluten-Free, Dairy-Free, Soy-Free

This Spiced Apple and Almond Crisp is a comforting and nourishing dessert that aligns perfectly with the Good Energy principles. The warm, spiced apples provide a natural sweetness and are packed with fiber, while the almond topping adds healthy fats and protein. This crisp is a delicious way to enjoy a treat that supports metabolic health and offers anti-inflammatory benefits. It's a guilt-free dessert that feels indulgent but is full of nutrients to keep you energized.

Prep time: 15 minutes | Cooking time: 30 minutes | Servings: 6

Ingredients:

- For the Apple Filling:
- 4 large apples (Granny Smith or Honeycrisp work well), peeled, cored, and sliced
- 1 tablespoon lemon juice
- 1/4 cup maple syrup
- 1 teaspoon ground cinnamon
- 1/2 teaspoon ground nutmeg
- 1/4 teaspoon ground ginger
- 1 teaspoon vanilla extract
- Pinch of sea salt
- For the Almond Crisp Topping:
- 1 cup almond flour
- 1/2 cup sliced almonds
- 1/4 cup coconut oil, melted
- 1/4 cup maple syrup
- 1/2 teaspoon ground cinnamon
- Pinch of sea salt

Step-by-Step Directions:

1. Prepare the Apple Filling: Mix the Apples: I begin by preheating the oven to 350°F (175°C). In a large mixing bowl, I combine the sliced apples with lemon juice, maple syrup, ground cinnamon, nutmeg, ginger, vanilla extract, and a pinch of sea salt. I toss everything together until the apples are evenly coated with the spices and sweetener.
2. Transfer to Baking Dish: I pour the apple mixture into a baking dish, spreading it out in an even layer.
3. Prepare the Almond Crisp Topping:
4. Mix the Topping: In a separate bowl, I mix the almond flour, sliced almonds, melted coconut oil, maple syrup, ground cinnamon, and a pinch of sea salt. I stir until the mixture forms a crumbly, moist topping.
5. Top the Apples: I sprinkle the almond crisp mixture evenly over the spiced apples in the baking dish, ensuring the apples are fully covered.
6. Bake the Crisp: I place the baking dish in the preheated oven and bake for 30-35 minutes, or until the topping is golden brown and the apples are tender. The kitchen will start to smell amazing as the spices and apples cook together.
7. Serve: Once the crisp is done baking, I remove it from the oven and let it cool slightly before serving. It's best enjoyed warm.

Nutritional Information (Per Serving):

- Calories: 250 | Protein: 4g | Fiber: 5g | Healthy Fats: 14g | Carbs: 28g

Tips:

1. Serving Suggestion: I love to serve this crisp with a scoop of dairy-free vanilla ice cream or a dollop of coconut yogurt for extra creaminess.
2. Storage: Leftovers can be stored in the refrigerator for up to 3 days. Reheat in the oven or microwave before serving.

Matcha Green Tea Coconut Ice Cream

Gluten-Free, Dairy-Free, Soy-Free

This Matcha Green Tea Coconut Ice Cream is a refreshing dessert that aligns perfectly with the Good Energy principles. The matcha provides a gentle energy boost with its natural caffeine and is rich in antioxidants, while the coconut milk offers healthy fats that support metabolism and keep you satisfied. This ice cream is both indulgent and nourishing, making it a great treat that won't derail your health goals.

Prep time: 15 minutes | Cooking time: None | Chill time: 4 hours (minimum) | Servings: 6

Ingredients:

- 2 cans (14 oz each) full-fat coconut milk
- 1/4 cup maple syrup
- 2 teaspoons matcha green tea powder
- 1 teaspoon vanilla extract
- Pinch of sea salt

Step-by-Step Directions:

1. Blend the Ingredients: Combine the Base: I start by shaking the cans of coconut milk well to ensure the fat is evenly distributed. Then, in a blender, I combine the coconut milk, maple syrup, matcha powder, vanilla extract, and a pinch of sea salt. I blend on high until the mixture is smooth and well combined, making sure there are no lumps of matcha powder.
2. Chill the Mixture: Refrigerate: After blending, I pour the mixture into a large bowl and cover it with plastic wrap. I then place it in the refrigerator to chill for at least 2 hours. Chilling the mixture ensures that it freezes evenly and develops a smooth texture when churned.
3. Churn the Ice Cream: Use an Ice Cream Maker: Once the mixture is thoroughly chilled, I transfer it to an ice cream maker and churn according to the manufacturer's instructions. This usually takes about 20-25 minutes, depending on your machine. The ice cream should be thick and creamy by the end of the churning process.
4. Freeze the Ice Cream: Final Freeze: I transfer the churned ice cream into a freezer-safe container, smoothing the top with a spatula. I cover the container with a lid and place it in the freezer for at least 2 more hours, or until it's firm enough to scoop.
5. Serve: Enjoy: Once the ice cream is fully set, I scoop it into bowls and serve. It's best enjoyed immediately, but you can store any leftovers in the freezer for up to a week.

Nutritional Information (Per Serving):

- Calories: 220 | Protein: 2g | Fiber: 1g | Healthy Fats: 18g | Carbs: 13g

Tips:

1. Storage: If the ice cream hardens too much in the freezer, let it sit at room temperature for about 10 minutes before scooping.
2. Variation: For an extra twist, you can add a tablespoon of shredded coconut or a handful of chopped dark chocolate into the mixture before churning.

Pumpkin Spice Chia Pudding

Gluten-Free, Dairy-Free, Soy-Free

This Pumpkin Spice Chia Pudding is the perfect way to enjoy the flavors of fall while staying true to the Good Energy principles. Rich in omega-3s, fiber, and antioxidants, this dessert not only satisfies your sweet tooth but also supports metabolic health and reduces inflammation. The warming spices combined with the creamy texture make this pudding a comforting yet healthy treat that can be enjoyed any time of day.

Prep time: 10 minutes | Cooking time: None | Chill time: 4 hours or overnight) | Servings: 4

Ingredients:

- 1 cup unsweetened almond milk (or your preferred dairy-free milk)
- 1/2 cup pumpkin puree (unsweetened)
- 1/4 cup chia seeds
- 2 tablespoons maple syrup (adjust to taste)
- 1 teaspoon vanilla extract
- 1 teaspoon ground cinnamon
- 1/2 teaspoon ground ginger
- 1/4 teaspoon ground nutmeg
- 1/4 teaspoon ground cloves
- Pinch of sea salt

Step-by-Step Directions:

1. Mix the Ingredients: In a medium-sized mixing bowl, I whisk together the almond milk, pumpkin puree, maple syrup, vanilla extract, and spices until everything is well combined. The mixture should be smooth and fragrant.
2. Add the Chia Seeds: Once the liquid mixture is ready, I stir in the chia seeds. I make sure the seeds are evenly distributed throughout the mixture to avoid clumping.
3. Chill the Pudding: After mixing, I cover the bowl with plastic wrap or transfer the mixture to individual serving jars. I then place it in the refrigerator to chill for at least 4 hours, but overnight is best. This allows the chia seeds to absorb the liquid and swell, creating a thick, pudding-like consistency.
4. Serve: Once the pudding has set, I give it a quick stir and serve it chilled. If it's in individual jars, it's ready to grab and enjoy.

Nutritional Information (Per Serving):

- Calories: 120 | Protein: 3g | Fiber: 6g | Healthy Fats: 4g | Carbs: 16g

Tips:

1. Texture: If you prefer a smoother texture, you can blend the mixture before chilling it to break down the chia seeds.
2. Toppings: I love to top this pudding with a sprinkle of cinnamon, a dollop of coconut yogurt, or a handful of toasted pecans for added crunch and flavor.

Serving Suggestions:

- This Pumpkin Spice Chia Pudding is perfect for a healthy dessert or a satisfying snack. It's also great for breakfast, especially when topped with some granola or fresh fruit. You can store it in the refrigerator for up to 5 days, making it an excellent option for meal prep.

Baked Apple Slices with Cinnamon and Almonds

Gluten-Free, Dairy-Free, Soy-Free

Baked Apple Slices with Cinnamon and Almonds is a delicious, warming dessert that perfectly fits the Good Energy lifestyle. This dish combines the natural sweetness of apples with the warmth of cinnamon and the crunch of almonds. It's rich in fiber, antioxidants, and healthy fats, making it a satisfying treat that supports metabolic health and promotes sustained energy.

Prep time: 10 minutes | Cooking time: 20 minutes | Servings: 4

Ingredients:

- 4 medium apples (such as Honeycrisp or Fuji), cored and sliced
- 1/4 cup sliced almonds
- 1 tbsp coconut oil, melted
- 1 tbsp ground cinnamon
- 1 tbsp pure maple syrup or honey (optional, for extra sweetness)
- 1/2 tsp vanilla extract
- A pinch of sea salt

Step-by-Step Directions:

1. Preheat the Oven: I'll start by preheating the oven to 375°F (190°C) and preparing a baking dish by lightly greasing it with a bit of coconut oil.
2. Prepare the Apple Slices: I'll core and slice the apples into even slices, ensuring they're not too thin to avoid overcooking. In a large mixing bowl, I'll toss the apple slices with the melted coconut oil, ground cinnamon, vanilla extract, and a pinch of sea salt. If I want a sweeter dessert, I can drizzle the apple slices with maple syrup or honey at this stage.
3. Bake the Apple Slices: I'll arrange the coated apple slices in a single layer in the prepared baking dish. Sprinkling the sliced almonds evenly over the top. I'll bake the apples in the preheated oven for about 20 minutes or until they're tender and the almonds are lightly toasted.
4. Serve: Once baked, I'll let the apple slices cool slightly before serving them warm.

Nutritional Information (Per Serving):

- Calories: 180 | Protein: 2g | Fiber: 4g | Healthy Fats: 7g | Carbs: 28g

Tips:

1. Apple Variety: I can use a mix of sweet and tart apples for a more complex flavor.
2. Add a Crunch: For added texture, I can top the apples with a handful of granola before baking.

Serving Suggestions:

- This dessert is perfect on its own or served with a dollop of coconut yogurt or a sprinkle of extra cinnamon. It's an excellent choice for a post-dinner treat that won't spike blood sugar levels, keeping energy steady and digestion smooth.

Chia Seed Pudding with Fresh Berries

Gluten-Free, Dairy-Free, Soy-Free

Chia Seed Pudding with Fresh Berries is a nutrient-packed dessert that aligns with the Good Energy principles. This pudding is rich in omega-3 fatty acids, fiber, and antioxidants, making it a perfect treat to support metabolic health, reduce inflammation, and maintain balanced energy levels throughout the day.

Prep time: 10 minutes | Chill time: 4 hours or overnight | Servings: 4

Ingredients:

- 1/2 cup chia seeds
- 2 cups unsweetened almond milk (or any other plant-based milk)
- 1 tsp pure vanilla extract
- 1 tbsp maple syrup or honey (optional, for added sweetness)
- 1/2 tsp ground cinnamon
- 1 cup mixed fresh berries (such as strawberries, blueberries, and raspberries)
- 1 tbsp unsweetened shredded coconut (optional, for topping)
- A pinch of sea salt

Step-by-Step Directions:

1. Prepare the Pudding Base: In a mixing bowl, I'll whisk together the chia seeds, almond milk, vanilla extract, maple syrup (if using), ground cinnamon, and a pinch of sea salt until everything is well combined.
2. Let the Pudding Set: I'll cover the bowl and place it in the refrigerator for at least 4 hours or overnight to allow the chia seeds to absorb the liquid and thicken into a pudding-like consistency. I'll make sure to stir the mixture after the first 30 minutes to prevent clumping.
3. Assemble the Pudding: Once the pudding has set, I'll give it a good stir to ensure it's smooth and evenly thickened. I'll then divide the pudding into four serving bowls or jars.
4. Add the Berries: I'll top each portion with a generous serving of mixed fresh berries. For added texture and flavor, I can sprinkle some unsweetened shredded coconut on top.
5. Serve: The pudding can be served immediately or stored in the refrigerator until ready to eat.

Nutritional Information (Per Serving):

- Calories: 200 | Protein: 4g | Fiber: 9g | Healthy Fats: 10g | Carbs: 20g

Tips:

1. Make It Ahead: This pudding is perfect for meal prep; I can make a big batch and enjoy it throughout the week.
2. Customize Your Pudding: For added flavor, I can mix in some cocoa powder or matcha powder with the chia seeds before setting the pudding.

Serving Suggestions:

- Chia Seed Pudding with Fresh Berries is delicious on its own, but I can also pair it with a handful of nuts or a spoonful of almond butter for added healthy fats and protein. This dessert is not only satisfying but also keeps energy levels stable and supports digestive health.

Coconut and Lime Energy Bites

Gluten-Free, Dairy-Free, Soy-Free

Coconut and Lime Energy Bites are a refreshing and nutritious dessert that perfectly aligns with the Good Energy principles. These bites are packed with healthy fats, fiber, and natural sweetness, making them an ideal snack to keep energy levels steady and support metabolic health.

Prep time: 15 minutes | Cooking time: 30 minutes | Servings: Makes 12 bites

Ingredients:

- 1 cup unsweetened shredded coconut
- 1/2 cup almond flour
- 2 tbsp coconut oil, melted
- 2 tbsp maple syrup or honey
- Zest of 2 limes
- Juice of 1 lime
- 1/4 tsp sea salt
- 1/2 tsp pure vanilla extract

Nutritional Information (Per Serving):

- Calories: 80 | Protein: 1g | Fiber: 2g | Healthy Fats: 7g | Carbs: 5g

Step-by-Step Directions:

1. Mix the Ingredients: In a mixing bowl, I'll combine the shredded coconut, almond flour, melted coconut oil, maple syrup (or honey), lime zest, lime juice, sea salt, and vanilla extract. I'll stir everything together until it forms a sticky, well-blended dough.
2. Form the Bites: Using my hands, I'll roll the mixture into small bite-sized balls, about 1 inch in diameter. If the mixture is too crumbly, I can add a little more lime juice or a small amount of water to help it stick together.
3. Chill the Bites: I'll place the energy bites on a baking sheet lined with parchment paper and refrigerate them for at least 30 minutes to firm up.
4. Serve: Once chilled, I'll transfer the energy bites to an airtight container. They can be stored in the refrigerator for up to a week or in the freezer for longer storage.

Tips:

1. For Extra Zing: I can roll the bites in additional shredded coconut or lime zest before chilling to add an extra burst of flavor and texture.
2. Nut-Free Option: If I need a nut-free version, I can replace the almond flour with sunflower seed flour.

Serving Suggestions:

- These Coconut and Lime Energy Bites are perfect as a quick snack, post-workout treat, or even as a light dessert. They pair well with a cup of herbal tea or a glass of sparkling water with a slice of lime.

DRINKS RECIPES
Matcha Green Tea with Almond Milk and Cinnamon
Gluten-Free, Dairy-Free, Soy-Free

This Matcha Green Tea with Almond Milk and Cinnamon is a delightful beverage that combines the antioxidant power of matcha with the creamy richness of almond milk and the warm, comforting flavor of cinnamon. This drink is designed to boost your energy levels and metabolism while providing a soothing, balanced experience. It's perfect for a mid-morning pick-me-up or an afternoon break that aligns with the Good Energy principles.

Prep time: 5 minutes | Servings: 1

Ingredients:

- 1 teaspoon matcha green tea powder
- 1/2 cup hot water (not boiling, about 175°F)
- 1/2 cup unsweetened almond milk
- 1/2 teaspoon ground cinnamon (plus extra for garnish)
- 1 teaspoon maple syrup (optional, for sweetness)
- 1/4 teaspoon vanilla extract (optional)

Step-by-Step Directions:

1. Prepare the Matcha: In a small bowl or cup, I sift the matcha powder to remove any lumps. Then, I add the hot water and whisk the matcha vigorously using a bamboo whisk or a small regular whisk until it becomes frothy and smooth. This step is key to ensuring the matcha is well-dissolved and creamy.
2. Heat the Almond Milk: In a small saucepan, I gently heat the almond milk over medium heat. If using, I also add the maple syrup and vanilla extract at this stage. I whisk occasionally to prevent it from scorching and to ensure it's well combined.
3. Combine and Serve: Once the almond milk is warm, I pour it into the matcha mixture. I then add the ground cinnamon and whisk again until everything is thoroughly mixed. If you prefer, you can use a frother to make the drink extra creamy.
4. Garnish and Enjoy: I pour the finished drink into my favorite mug and sprinkle a little extra cinnamon on top. Now, it's ready to enjoy!

Nutritional Information (Per Serving):

- Calories: 60 | Protein: 2g | Fiber: 1g | Healthy Fats: 3g | Carbs: 6g

Tips:

1. Sweetness: If you like your drink a bit sweeter, feel free to adjust the amount of maple syrup or use a natural sweetener like stevia.
2. Iced Option: For a refreshing iced version, I let the matcha mixture cool and then pour it over ice. It's perfect for warmer days!

Serving Suggestions:

- This Matcha Green Tea with Almond Milk and Cinnamon is ideal on its own, but you can pair it with a light snack like a handful of nuts or a piece of fruit. It's a versatile drink that can be enjoyed any time of day, offering a gentle energy boost without the jitters.

Cucumber and Mint Infused Water

Gluten-Free, Dairy-Free, Soy-Free, Nut-Free

This Cucumber and Mint Infused Water is a refreshing and hydrating drink that aligns perfectly with the Good Energy principles. It's light, revitalizing, and packed with natural ingredients that help boost metabolism and support overall health. The cucumber provides a subtle, cooling flavor, while the mint adds a fresh, invigorating note. This drink is a great way to stay hydrated and energized throughout the day.

Prep time: 5 minutes | Servings: 2

Ingredients:

- 1/2 cucumber, thinly sliced
- 10 fresh mint leaves
- 4 cups filtered water
- Ice cubes (optional)

Step-by-Step Directions:

1. Prepare the Ingredients: I start by washing the cucumber and mint leaves thoroughly. Then, I slice the cucumber into thin rounds and gently bruise the mint leaves by pressing them between my fingers. This helps release their natural oils and flavor.
2. Combine in a Pitcher: In a large pitcher, I add the cucumber slices and mint leaves. Next, I pour in the filtered water, making sure the ingredients are well-submerged. If I want the drink to be extra cold, I'll add a few ice cubes.
3. Infuse the Water: I let the water sit in the refrigerator for at least 1 hour to allow the flavors to infuse. The longer it sits, the more pronounced the flavors will be. For a more intense taste, I might even leave it overnight.
4. Serve: When I'm ready to enjoy the infused water, I give it a gentle stir and pour it into glasses. If I'm serving guests, I might garnish each glass with a cucumber slice or a sprig of fresh mint for an elegant touch.

Nutritional Information (Per Serving):

- Calories: 5 | Carbs: 1g | Fiber: 0g | Fat: 0g | Protein: 0g

Tips:

1. Flavor Variations: You can experiment with adding other fresh herbs like basil or a squeeze of lemon or lime for additional flavor.
2. Refreshing Twist: For a bubbly version, I sometimes replace half of the water with sparkling water just before serving.

Serving Suggestions:

- This Cucumber and Mint Infused Water is perfect for sipping throughout the day to stay hydrated. It pairs well with light meals, especially salads, and is a great choice for a post-workout refresher. You can keep it in the refrigerator for up to 2 days, though it's best enjoyed fresh.
- This simple yet effective drink not only quenches your thirst but also supports your body's natural detoxification processes, making it a fantastic addition to your daily routine. It's an easy way to maintain your energy levels and stay refreshed, all while sticking to the Good Energy principles.

Anti-Inflammatory Turmeric Latte

Gluten-Free, Dairy-Free, Soy-Free

This Anti-Inflammatory Turmeric Latte is a warm, soothing drink that aligns with the Good Energy principles. It's packed with powerful ingredients like turmeric, which is renowned for its anti-inflammatory properties, and ginger, which supports digestion. Combined with creamy almond milk and a hint of cinnamon, this latte is not only delicious but also a perfect way to start or end your day with a boost of wellness.

Prep time: 5 minutes | Servings: 1

Ingredients:

- 1 cup unsweetened almond milk
- 1 teaspoon ground turmeric
- 1/2 teaspoon ground ginger
- 1/2 teaspoon ground cinnamon
- 1 teaspoon coconut oil (optional, for added creaminess)
- 1 teaspoon maple syrup or honey (optional, for sweetness)
- Pinch of black pepper (enhances turmeric absorption)
- 1/4 teaspoon vanilla extract (optional)

Step-by-Step Directions:

1. Heat the Almond Milk: I begin by pouring the almond milk into a small saucepan. I set it over medium heat and let it warm up gently. I don't want it to boil, just to become hot enough to dissolve the spices.
2. Add the Spices: Once the almond milk is warm, I whisk in the ground turmeric, ginger, and cinnamon. If I'm using coconut oil for extra creaminess, I add it at this stage. The black pepper is crucial as it enhances the absorption of curcumin, the active compound in turmeric, so I always include it.
3. Sweeten and Flavor: At this point, I stir in the maple syrup or honey if I want a touch of sweetness. I also add the vanilla extract if I'm using it. I keep whisking until everything is well combined and the latte has a beautiful golden color.
4. Simmer: I let the mixture simmer for a minute or two, allowing the flavors to meld together. This step also helps to slightly thicken the latte, making it more comforting and satisfying.
5. Serve: I pour the latte into my favorite mug, making sure to get all the creamy goodness. Sometimes, I sprinkle a little extra cinnamon on top for garnish.

Nutritional Information (Per Serving):

- Calories: 80 | Fat: 5g | Carbs: 8g | Fiber: 2g | Protein: 1g

Tips:

1. Customization: Feel free to adjust the spices to your liking. If you prefer a spicier kick, you can add a pinch more ginger or even a dash of cayenne pepper.
2. Storage: If I make a larger batch, I can store it in the fridge and reheat it for later, though it's best enjoyed fresh.

Serving Suggestions:

- This Turmeric Latte is perfect on its own, especially as a relaxing evening drink. It can also be paired with a light snack like a handful of nuts or a slice of gluten-free toast. It's a great way to unwind and provide your body with a dose of anti-inflammatory goodness.

Berry and Ginger Detox Smoothie

Gluten-Free, Dairy-Free, Soy-Free

This Berry and Ginger Detox Smoothie is a refreshing and revitalizing drink that perfectly aligns with the Good Energy principles. Packed with antioxidant-rich berries and anti-inflammatory ginger, this smoothie is designed to support metabolic health and promote detoxification. The combination of vibrant fruits and the zesty kick of ginger makes this a delicious way to start your day or recharge in the afternoon.

Prep time: 5 minutes | Servings: 2

Ingredients:

- 1 cup mixed berries (strawberries, blueberries, raspberries)
- 1/2 cup frozen cauliflower florets (for added creaminess and fiber)
- 1 small piece of fresh ginger (about 1 inch), peeled and grated
- 1 tablespoon chia seeds (for fiber and omega-3s)
- 1 tablespoon lemon juice (for a detoxifying boost)
- 1/2 cup coconut water (for hydration and electrolytes)
- 1/2 cup unsweetened almond milk (or any dairy-free milk)
- 1 teaspoon honey or maple syrup (optional, for sweetness)

Step-by-Step Directions:

1. Prepare the Ingredients: I start by gathering all the ingredients. I ensure the berries are washed and ready to go, the ginger is peeled and grated, and the chia seeds are measured out.
2. Blend the Ingredients: In a high-speed blender, I combine the mixed berries, frozen cauliflower florets, grated ginger, chia seeds, lemon juice, coconut water, and almond milk. If I want a touch of sweetness, I add the honey or maple syrup at this stage.
3. Blend Until Smooth: I blend everything on high speed until the mixture is smooth and creamy. The frozen cauliflower helps thicken the smoothie without altering the flavor, while the ginger adds a refreshing zing.
4. Serve: I pour the smoothie into two glasses, ensuring each serving is evenly distributed. Sometimes, I like to garnish the top with a few extra berries or a sprinkle of chia seeds for a bit of texture.

Nutritional Information (Per Serving):

- Calories: 120 | Fat: 4g | Carbs: 20g | Fiber: 8g | Protein: 3g

Tips:

1. Customization: You can adjust the amount of ginger based on your preference. If you're new to ginger, start with a smaller piece and increase as you get used to its flavor.
2. Boost It: For an extra detoxifying effect, add a handful of spinach or kale to the smoothie. You won't taste the greens, but you'll benefit from the added nutrients.

Serving Suggestions:

- This smoothie is a great way to start your morning with a burst of energy and detoxifying benefits. It's also perfect as a mid-day pick-me-up or a refreshing post-workout drink. Pair it with a handful of nuts or a light snack if you need something more substantial.

Golden Milk Turmeric Latte

Gluten-Free, Dairy-Free, Soy-Free

The Golden Milk Turmeric Latte is a warm, soothing drink that embodies the principles of Good Energy by harnessing the anti-inflammatory power of turmeric combined with the creamy richness of coconut milk. This latte is designed to support metabolic health, reduce inflammation, and promote overall well-being. It's the perfect drink to start or end your day on a healthy note.

Prep time: 5 minutes | Servings: 2

Ingredients:

- 1 cup unsweetened coconut milk (or any dairy-free milk of your choice)
- 1 teaspoon ground turmeric (for its anti-inflammatory properties)
- 1/2 teaspoon ground cinnamon (for blood sugar regulation)
- 1/4 teaspoon ground ginger (for digestion and anti-inflammatory benefits)
- 1/4 teaspoon vanilla extract (optional, for flavor)
- 1 teaspoon honey or maple syrup (optional, for a touch of sweetness)
- A pinch of black pepper (to enhance turmeric absorption)
- A pinch of ground nutmeg (optional, for extra warmth)

Step-by-Step Directions:

1. Heat the Milk: I begin by pouring the coconut milk into a small saucepan. I heat it over medium-low heat, making sure not to let it boil, just until it's warm.
2. Add the Spices: As the milk warms, I whisk in the ground turmeric, cinnamon, ginger, black pepper, and nutmeg (if using). I stir continuously to ensure the spices are fully incorporated into the milk.
3. Sweeten and Flavor: Once the spices are well mixed, I add the vanilla extract and honey or maple syrup if I want a bit of sweetness. I continue stirring until everything is well combined and the milk is hot.
4. Serve: I pour the latte into two small mugs. The rich yellow color from the turmeric is visually stunning, and the warm spices create a comforting aroma.

Nutritional Information (Per Serving):

- Calories: 90 | Fat: 7g | Carbs: 6g | Fiber: 1g | Protein: 1g

Tips:

1. Enhancing Absorption: The black pepper is crucial as it significantly boosts the absorption of curcumin, the active ingredient in turmeric.
2. Adjust Sweetness: You can adjust the amount of honey or maple syrup to your taste or omit it entirely if you prefer an unsweetened drink.
3. Extra Creamy: For a richer texture, you can use full-fat coconut milk.

Serving Suggestions:

- This Golden Milk Turmeric Latte is perfect for sipping in the evening as a calming bedtime ritual or in the morning to start your day with an anti-inflammatory boost. It pairs well with a light snack, like a piece of fruit or a handful of nuts.

Green Detox Juice with Spinach, Cucumber, and Ginger

Gluten-Free, Dairy-Free, Soy-Free

This Green Detox Juice is packed with ingredients that are known for their detoxifying and anti-inflammatory properties. The combination of spinach, cucumber, and ginger creates a refreshing drink that supports metabolic health, aids digestion, and promotes overall vitality. It's the perfect drink to kickstart your day or give you a midday boost.

Prep time: 10 minutes | Servings: 2

Ingredients:

- 1 cup fresh spinach leaves (rich in antioxidants and vitamins)
- 1 medium cucumber (hydrating and low in calories)
- 1 green apple (adds natural sweetness and fiber)
- 1/2 inch fresh ginger root (anti-inflammatory and aids digestion)
- Juice of 1/2 lemon (boosts vitamin C and aids in detoxification)
- 1/2 cup water (adjust for consistency)
- Ice cubes (optional, for serving)

Step-by-Step Directions:

1. Prepare the Ingredients: I start by washing all the fresh produce thoroughly. I then chop the cucumber, apple, and ginger into smaller pieces that will be easier to blend.
2. Blend the Ingredients: I add the spinach, cucumber, apple, ginger, and lemon juice into a high-speed blender. Next, I pour in the water to help everything blend smoothly. I blend on high until the mixture is smooth and well-combined.
3. Strain (Optional): If you prefer a smoother juice, you can pour the mixture through a fine-mesh strainer or nut milk bag to remove the pulp. I personally like to keep the fiber in for added health benefits.
4. Serve: I pour the juice into two small glasses over ice if I want it chilled. The vibrant green color is a visual treat, and the fresh aroma of ginger and lemon is invigorating.

Nutritional Information (Per Serving):

- Calories: 60 | Fat: 0.5g | Carbs: 14g | Fiber: 3g | Protein: 1g

Tips:

1. Boost the Detox: Adding a handful of fresh parsley or a stalk of celery can enhance the detoxifying effects.
2. Adjust the Sweetness: If you prefer a sweeter juice, you can add another half of an apple or a small piece of pineapple.

Serving Suggestions:

- This Green Detox Juice is perfect to enjoy first thing in the morning on an empty stomach or as a refreshing drink in the afternoon. It pairs well with a light snack like a handful of nuts or a boiled egg for a balanced energy boost.

This juice is not only refreshing but also a powerful way to flood your body with nutrients, supporting your health and energy throughout the day. It's an easy and delicious way to stay aligned with the Good Energy principles.

Hibiscus and Rosehip Iced Tea

Gluten-Free, Dairy-Free, Soy-Free

This Hibiscus and Rosehip Iced Tea is a refreshing and invigorating drink that combines the tangy flavors of hibiscus with the subtle floral notes of rosehip. Both hibiscus and rosehip are rich in antioxidants and vitamin C, making this iced tea a perfect choice for boosting your immune system and supporting metabolic health. It's a delicious way to stay hydrated while enjoying a drink that's aligned with the principles of Good Energy.

Prep time: 10 minutes (plus steeping time) | Servings: 2

Ingredients:

- 2 tablespoons dried hibiscus flowers (rich in antioxidants, supports cardiovascular health)
- 1 tablespoon dried rosehip (high in vitamin C, supports immune function)
- 3 cups water (filtered, for the base of the tea)
- 1-2 teaspoons honey or agave syrup (optional, for sweetness)
- Ice cubes (for serving)
- Fresh mint leaves or lemon slices (optional, for garnish)

Step-by-Step Directions:

1. Boil the Water: I start by bringing 3 cups of water to a boil in a medium-sized pot. As it heats up, I prepare the dried hibiscus flowers and rosehip by placing them in a heatproof teapot or large jar.
2. Steep the Tea: Once the water reaches a rolling boil, I pour it over the hibiscus and rosehip in the teapot. I let the mixture steep for about 10 minutes, allowing the flavors to fully infuse and the color to deepen.
3. Strain and Sweeten: After steeping, I strain the tea into a large pitcher to remove the flowers and rosehip. If you prefer a slightly sweeter tea, this is when you can stir in honey or agave syrup to taste. I mix it well until the sweetener dissolves completely.
4. Chill and Serve: I let the tea cool to room temperature before placing it in the refrigerator to chill for at least 30 minutes. When I'm ready to serve, I pour the iced tea into glasses filled with ice cubes. For an extra touch, I like to garnish each glass with fresh mint leaves or a slice of lemon.

Nutritional Information (Per Serving):

- Calories: 20 | Fat: 0g | Carbs: 5g | Fiber: 0g | Protein: 0g

Tips:

1. Customize the Flavor: If you want a more robust flavor, increase the steeping time or the amount of hibiscus and rosehip used.
2. Herbal Variations: You can experiment by adding other herbs like lavender or chamomile for a different twist.

Serving Suggestions:

- This Hibiscus and Rosehip Iced Tea is perfect for a midday refreshment or a light, cooling drink on a warm day. Pair it with a light snack like almond flour crackers or a fresh fruit salad for a balanced, energy-boosting treat.

Enjoy this iced tea as a naturally flavorful way to stay hydrated and energized, fully in line with the Good Energy principles. It's a simple yet powerful drink that supports your overall well-being.

Blueberry and Basil Infused Water

Gluten-Free, Dairy-Free, Soy-Free, Nut-Free

This Blueberry and Basil Infused Water is a refreshing and simple drink that elevates plain water with the natural sweetness of blueberries and the aromatic touch of fresh basil. Blueberries are packed with antioxidants, while basil offers anti-inflammatory properties, making this drink both hydrating and supportive of metabolic health. It's a perfect way to enjoy water with a hint of flavor that aligns with the Good Energy principles.

Prep time: 5 minutes (plus infusion time) | Servings: 2

Ingredients:

- 1 cup fresh blueberries (rich in antioxidants, supports brain health)
- 5-6 fresh basil leaves (anti-inflammatory, aids digestion)
- 4 cups filtered water (the base for infusion)

Step-by-Step Directions:

1. Prepare the Ingredients: I begin by rinsing the blueberries and basil leaves thoroughly under cool water. Once cleaned, I lightly crush the blueberries using the back of a spoon to help release their juices, which will infuse the water with more flavor.
2. Combine in a Pitcher: I add the crushed blueberries and basil leaves to a large pitcher, then pour in the 4 cups of filtered water. I give it a gentle stir to mix everything together.
3. Infuse the Water: I cover the pitcher and place it in the refrigerator for at least 2 hours, allowing the flavors to infuse fully. For a stronger flavor, I might let it sit overnight.
4. Serve: When it's ready, I pour the infused water into glasses. Sometimes I add a few extra fresh blueberries and a basil leaf to each glass for a pretty presentation.

Nutritional Information (Per Serving):

- Calories: 5 | Fat: 0g | Carbs: 1g | Fiber: 0g | Protein: 0g

Tips:

1. Adjust the Intensity: If you prefer a more intense flavor, you can gently muddle the basil leaves before adding them to the water.
2. Keep It Cool: For an even more refreshing experience, serve the infused water over ice.

Serving Suggestions:

- This Blueberry and Basil Infused Water is a perfect companion for meals or as a refreshing drink throughout the day. Pair it with a light snack like cucumber and carrot sticks with a spicy tahini dip for a healthy, energy-boosting treat.

This infused water is a deliciously simple way to stay hydrated while supporting your overall health and well-being, perfectly fitting the Good Energy lifestyle.

Almond and Cinnamon Spiced Coffee

Gluten-Free, Dairy-Free, Soy-Free

This Almond and Cinnamon Spiced Coffee is a warm and comforting beverage that blends the richness of almond milk with the sweet and spicy notes of cinnamon. Both ingredients are known for their anti-inflammatory properties and can help stabilize blood sugar levels, making this a perfect morning or afternoon pick-me-up that aligns with the principles of Good Energy.

Prep time: 5 minutes | Servings: 2

Ingredients:

- 2 cups almond milk (unsweetened, dairy-free, rich in vitamin E)
- 1 tablespoon ground coffee (provides energy, antioxidants)
- 1/2 teaspoon ground cinnamon (anti-inflammatory, helps regulate blood sugar)
- 1 teaspoon coconut sugar or honey (optional, adds natural sweetness)

Step-by-Step Directions:

1. Brew the Coffee: I start by brewing a strong cup of coffee using your preferred method. For this recipe, I use a French press, adding 1 tablespoon of ground coffee to the press and pouring in 1 cup of hot water. After letting it steep for about 4 minutes, I press down the plunger.
2. Heat the Almond Milk: While the coffee is brewing, I heat the almond milk in a small saucepan over medium heat. I add the ground cinnamon and whisk it into the milk, ensuring it's well combined.
3. Combine and Sweeten: Once the almond milk is heated and frothy, I pour the brewed coffee into two mugs, then top each with the warm almond milk. If you like a little sweetness, you can stir in a teaspoon of coconut sugar or honey at this stage.
4. Serve: I finish by sprinkling a pinch of extra cinnamon on top of each mug for a bit of extra flavor and aroma.

Nutritional Information (Per Serving):

- Calories: 40 | Fat: 2.5g | Carbs: 4g | Fiber: 1g | Protein: 1g

Tips:

1. Froth It Up: If you have a milk frother, use it to froth the almond milk before adding it to the coffee for a café-style experience.
2. Go Decaf: If you prefer to avoid caffeine, use decaffeinated coffee instead.

Serving Suggestions:

- This Almond and Cinnamon Spiced Coffee pairs beautifully with a light breakfast or snack, such as almond flour crackers with olive tapenade, for a satisfying start to your day.

Cucumber-Lemon Detox Water

Gluten-Free, Dairy-Free, Soy-Free, Nut-Free

Cucumber-Lemon Detox Water is a refreshing and hydrating drink that fits perfectly within the Good Energy principles. This drink is designed to support metabolism, promote hydration, and provide a gentle detoxification with natural ingredients. It's a simple yet effective way to keep the body energized and refreshed throughout the day.

Prep time: 5 minutes | Servings: 2

Ingredients:

- 1/2 cucumber, thinly sliced
- 1/2 lemon, thinly sliced
- 4 cups filtered water
- 4-5 fresh mint leaves (optional)
- Ice cubes (optional)

Step-by-Step Directions:

1. Prepare the Ingredients: I'll start by thinly slicing the cucumber and lemon. If I'm using mint leaves, I'll gently bruise them with my fingers to release their natural oils.
2. Assemble the Detox Water: In a large pitcher, I'll add the cucumber slices, lemon slices, and mint leaves. Then, I'll pour in the filtered water.
3. Chill and Infuse: I'll let the water infuse in the refrigerator for at least 30 minutes to allow the flavors to blend. For a more intense flavor, I can let it infuse for up to 2 hours.
4. Serve: I'll serve the detox water chilled, adding a few ice cubes if desired. The water can be stored in the refrigerator for up to 24 hours.

Nutritional Information (Per Serving):

- Calories: 5 | Protein: 0g | Fiber: 0.5g | Healthy Fats: 0g | Carbs: 1g

Tips:

1. Add a Twist: For an added detox boost, I can include a few slices of fresh ginger or a dash of apple cider vinegar.
2. Flavor Variations: I can experiment with other fruits or herbs like strawberries, basil, or lime to customize the flavor to my liking.

Serving Suggestions:

- This Cucumber-Lemon Detox Water is best enjoyed first thing in the morning or throughout the day to stay hydrated and refreshed. It's an excellent alternative to sugary drinks and helps to maintain optimal energy levels.

Minted Green Iced Tea

Gluten-Free, Dairy-Free, Soy-Free, Nut-Free

Minted Green Iced Tea is a refreshing, antioxidant-rich beverage that aligns perfectly with the Good Energy principles. This drink is designed to boost metabolism, support hydration, and provide a cooling, invigorating experience. With the benefits of green tea and fresh mint, it's a revitalizing choice for maintaining balanced energy throughout the day.

Prep time: 10 minutes | Servings: 2

Ingredients:

- 2 green tea bags
- 4 cups of filtered water
- 1/4 cup fresh mint leaves
- 1 tablespoon honey or maple syrup (optional)
- Ice cubes
- Lemon slices for garnish (optional)

Step-by-Step Directions:

1. Brew the Green Tea: I'll start by boiling 4 cups of filtered water. Once boiling, I'll remove it from heat and add the green tea bags. I'll let them steep for about 3-5 minutes, depending on how strong I want the tea.
2. Add Mint and Sweetener: While the tea is still hot, I'll add the fresh mint leaves to infuse their flavor. If I'm using a sweetener like honey or maple syrup, I'll stir it in now until it's fully dissolved.
3. Cool the Tea: I'll let the tea cool down to room temperature. Once cooled, I'll remove the tea bags and mint leaves.
4. Chill the Tea: I'll pour the tea into a pitcher and refrigerate it for at least 1-2 hours to chill.
5. Serve: To serve, I'll fill glasses with ice cubes, pour the minted green tea over the ice, and garnish with lemon slices if desired.

Nutritional Information (Per Serving):

- Calories: 5 | Protein: 0g | Fiber: 0g | Healthy Fats: 0g | Carbs: 1g (without sweetener)

Tips:

1. Adjust Sweetness: I can adjust the sweetness to taste or omit it entirely for a pure, unsweetened version.
2. Mint Variations: I could also experiment with other herbs like basil or rosemary for a different flavor profile.

Serving Suggestions:

- Minted Green Iced Tea is ideal as a midday refreshment or paired with meals. Its light and refreshing taste make it a perfect drink to stay hydrated while benefiting from the antioxidants in green tea.

Spiced Golden Milk with Coconut Milk

Gluten-Free, Dairy-Free, Soy-Free

Spiced Golden Milk with Coconut Milk is a warm, soothing drink that combines the anti-inflammatory benefits of turmeric with the richness of coconut milk. This recipe aligns with the Good Energy principles, promoting metabolic health and balanced nutrition. The blend of spices not only adds depth of flavor but also supports digestion and overall well-being.

Prep time: 5 minutes | Servings: 2

Ingredients:

- 2 cups of unsweetened coconut milk
- 1 teaspoon ground turmeric
- 1/2 teaspoon ground cinnamon
- 1/4 teaspoon ground ginger
- 1/8 teaspoon black pepper
- 1 tablespoon maple syrup or honey (optional)
- 1/2 teaspoon vanilla extract (optional)

Step-by-Step Directions:

1. Heat the Coconut Milk: I'll pour the coconut milk into a small saucepan and place it over medium heat. I'll warm it gently, making sure it doesn't boil.
2. Add the Spices: Once the milk is warm, I'll whisk in the turmeric, cinnamon, ginger, and black pepper. I'll continue to whisk until the spices are fully incorporated and the milk takes on a golden hue.
3. Sweeten and Flavor: If I prefer a touch of sweetness, I'll add the maple syrup or honey and the vanilla extract at this stage, whisking until everything is well combined.
4. Simmer: I'll let the mixture simmer on low heat for about 5 minutes to allow the flavors to meld together, stirring occasionally.
5. Serve: I'll pour the golden milk into mugs and enjoy it warm. It's a perfect drink for winding down in the evening or as a comforting morning beverage.

Tips:

1. Adjust Spice Levels: I can tweak the amount of spices to suit my taste. For a spicier kick, I might add a pinch of cayenne pepper.
2. Optional Froth: For a frothy finish, I could blend the golden milk in a blender for a few seconds before serving.

Nutritional Information (Per Serving):

- Calories: 130 | Protein: 1g | Fiber: 1g | Healthy Fats: 12g | Carbs: 6g

Serving Suggestions:

- This Spiced Golden Milk is best enjoyed warm and can be paired with a light snack like a handful of nuts or a slice of gluten-free toast. It's also a great pre-bedtime drink due to its calming properties.

How to Plan a Week of Good Energy Meals

Planning a week of meals that keep you energized and feeling your best doesn't have to be complicated. In fact, with a little bit of forethought, it can be a game-changer. When I first started focusing on eating for Good Energy, I realized that planning was key to staying on track and making sure I always had something nourishing to eat, even on the busiest days. Let me walk you through how I like to plan out my week of Good Energy meals.

1. Start with Your Schedule

The first thing I do is take a look at my week ahead. I consider which days are going to be hectic and which ones might give me more time to cook. On busy days, I plan for meals that are quick and easy or that can be made ahead of time. For the days when I have more time, I might choose to experiment with a new recipe or cook something a bit more elaborate. This way, I'm never scrambling to figure out what to eat when things get crazy.

2. Mix and Match Recipes

Next, I like to mix up my meals so that I'm not eating the same thing every day. I choose a variety of breakfast, lunch, and dinner recipes that align with the Good Energy principles—whole, unprocessed foods, balanced macronutrients, and anti-inflammatory ingredients. I make sure there's a good balance of protein, healthy fats, and complex carbs across all my meals. I'll usually pick two or three breakfast options that I can rotate throughout the week, along with a few different lunch and dinner ideas. Snacks are simple—things like roasted nuts, fresh fruit, or a quick veggie dip.

3. Make a Grocery List

Once I've planned out my meals, I make a detailed grocery list. I find it helpful to group items by category—produce, proteins, pantry staples, etc.—to make shopping more efficient. This also helps ensure I don't forget anything, so I'm not running back to the store mid-week. I love keeping things organized, and a good list is the first step in making meal prep go smoothly.

4. Prep What You Can Ahead of Time

On Sunday or another day when I have some free time, I do as much prep work as possible. I might chop vegetables, cook grains like quinoa or brown rice, and even batch-cook proteins like grilled chicken or roasted chickpeas. Having these components ready to go makes it so much easier to throw together a meal during the week. Plus, it cuts down on the temptation to reach for something less nutritious when you're in a hurry.

5. Plan for Leftovers

I always make a little extra when I cook dinner so that I have leftovers for lunch the next day. Not only does this save time, but it also ensures that I'm eating well even when I'm short on time. Leftovers are your friend when it comes to maintaining Good Energy throughout the week. I like to think of it as cooking once, eating twice!

6. Stay Flexible

Life happens, and sometimes plans change. I've learned to stay flexible and not stress if things don't go exactly as planned. Maybe I swap out a meal or two, or I end up going out to eat one night. The important thing is to do your best and make choices that support your energy and well-being. Planning is about setting yourself up for success, but it doesn't have to be rigid.

Tips for Efficient Meal Prep

Meal prep has become one of my secret weapons for staying on track with my Good Energy lifestyle. When you take the time to prep in advance, you save yourself from the stress of figuring out what to eat during the week. Plus, it's a great way to make sure you're eating nutrient-dense meals that keep your energy levels steady. Here are some of my favorite tips for making meal prep as efficient and enjoyable as possible.

1. Keep It Simple

When I first started meal prepping, I tried to do too much at once, and it quickly became overwhelming. Now, I keep it simple. I choose a few key ingredients that I can mix and match throughout the week—like a batch of roasted veggies, some cooked grains, and a versatile protein like grilled chicken or tofu. These basics can be turned into different meals depending on what I'm in the mood for.

2. Use Your Freezer

The freezer is your best friend when it comes to meal prep. I like to double recipes and freeze half for later. Soups, stews, and casseroles all freeze well, and having them on hand means I've always got a healthy meal ready to go, even when I'm short on time. I also like to freeze portions of cooked grains and beans, which can easily be added to a dish without any extra cooking.

3. Invest in Good Containers

Having the right containers makes a huge difference in how easy and efficient meal prep can be. I use glass containers with tight-fitting lids for storing prepped ingredients and meals. They keep food fresh longer and make it easy to see what I have ready to eat. Mason jars are also great for storing salads or smoothies that I can grab and go.

4. Multitask While Cooking

When I'm cooking, I try to make the most of my time by multitasking. For example, I might roast veggies in the oven while cooking grains on the stovetop. Or I'll prep a salad while a soup simmers. By doing multiple things at once, I can get more done in less time, which means I'm spending less time in the kitchen overall.

5. Get the Family Involved

Meal prep doesn't have to be a solo activity. I love getting the family involved, whether it's having the kids help wash and chop vegetables or asking my partner to grill some chicken while I prepare other dishes. It's a great way to spend time together and make healthy eating a family affair.

6. Label Everything

This might sound a bit obsessive, but labeling your prepped meals and ingredients can save you a lot of hassle. I label containers with the date they were prepped and what's inside, so I always know what needs to be used up first. It also helps prevent any mystery containers from getting lost in the fridge.

7. Clean as You Go

One of my top tips for making meal prep less daunting is to clean as you go. Instead of letting dirty dishes pile up, I wash them as I'm cooking. This keeps the kitchen from turning into a disaster zone and makes the whole process feel a lot more manageable.

With these tips, you'll find meal prep can be a fun and rewarding part of your weekly routine. Not only will you save time and stress during the week, but you'll also have the peace of mind knowing that you're fueling your body with the best possible foods. Here's to a week of Good Energy!

GOOD ENERGY FOOD LISTS

When you're aiming to cook and live according to the Good Energy principles, having a well-planned shopping list is crucial. Here's a comprehensive guide to your Good Energy food shopping lists, organized by category to help you easily navigate the grocery store and stock your kitchen with nutrient-dense, anti-inflammatory, and metabolism-boosting ingredients.

Fresh Produce

Leafy Greens: Spinach, kale, arugula, collard greens, Swiss chard

Cruciferous Vegetables: Broccoli, cauliflower, Brussels sprouts, cabbage

Root Vegetables: Sweet potatoes, carrots, beets, parsnips

Alliums: Garlic, onions, leeks, shallots

Fruits: Berries (blueberries, strawberries, raspberries), apples, pears, citrus fruits (lemons, limes, oranges), avocados

Other Vegetables: Zucchini, bell peppers, cucumbers, tomatoes, asparagus, mushrooms, eggplant

Herbs: Fresh basil, parsley, cilantro, thyme, rosemary, mint, dill

Whole Grains & Pseudograins

Quinoa

Buckwheat

Amaranth

Millet

Brown rice

Gluten-free oats

Healthy Fats

Avocados

Olive oil (extra virgin)

Coconut oil

Nuts: Almonds, walnuts, cashews, pecans

Seeds: Chia seeds, flaxseeds, hemp seeds, pumpkin seeds

Nut Butters: Almond butter, cashew butter, sunflower seed butter

Protein Sources

Legumes: Lentils, chickpeas, black beans, white beans

Fish: Salmon, sardines, mackerel (wild-caught)

Poultry: Organic chicken, turkey

Eggs: Free-range, organic eggs

Tofu and Tempeh: (For those who consume soy)

Grass-Fed Meat: Beef, lamb (optional)

Nutritional Yeast: For a cheesy flavor and added B vitamins

Dairy Alternatives

Coconut milk (unsweetened)

Almond milk (unsweetened)

Oat milk (unsweetened)

Coconut yogurt (unsweetened)

Pantry Staples

Spices: Turmeric, cinnamon, cumin, paprika, chili powder, black pepper, sea salt, garlic powder, ginger powder

Condiments: Apple cider vinegar, balsamic vinegar, coconut aminos, Dijon mustard, tahini

Broths: Vegetable broth, bone broth (low-sodium)

Flours: Almond flour, coconut flour, cassava flour

Sweeteners: Raw honey, maple syrup, dates

Frozen Foods

Frozen Berries: Blueberries, raspberries, strawberries

Frozen Vegetables: Spinach, peas, broccoli, cauliflower rice

Frozen Fish: Salmon, cod, shrimp (wild-caught)

Snacks

Raw nuts and seeds

Dried fruits: Unsweetened apricots, raisins, dates

Dark chocolate (70% cacao or higher)

Rice cakes

Kale chips

Seaweed snacks

Drinks

Herbal teas: Green tea, chamomile, peppermint, ginger tea

Coconut water (unsweetened)

Sparkling water (unsweetened)

Cold-pressed juices: Green juice, beet juice

Optional Superfoods

Maca powder

Spirulina

Chlorella

Cacao nibs

Collagen peptides

This shopping list is designed to ensure your kitchen is stocked with ingredients that support the Good Energy lifestyle. The items listed will allow you to create meals that are not only delicious and satisfying but also promote metabolic health, reduce inflammation, and sustain your energy levels throughout the day.

30-DAY MEAL PLAN

Day 1

Breakfast: Quinoa Breakfast Bowl with Blueberries and Almond Butter

Lunch: Grilled Chicken and Avocado Salad with Lemon-Basil Vinaigrette

Dinner: Roasted Chicken with Sweet Potatoes and Brussels Sprouts

Dessert: Raw Cacao and Avocado Mousse

Day 2

Breakfast: Smoked Salmon and Avocado Omelette

Lunch: Lentil and Kale Salad with Lemon-Tahini Dressing

Dinner: Lemon-Garlic Shrimp with Zucchini Noodles

Dessert: Coconut and Lime Energy Bites

Day 3

Breakfast: Almond Butter and Banana Smoothie

Lunch: Mediterranean Chickpea Salad with Cucumber and Feta

Dinner: Grass-Fed Beef Stir-Fry with Broccoli and Cauliflower Rice

Dessert: Baked Apple Slices with Cinnamon and Almonds

Day 4

Breakfast: Pumpkin-Spiced Quinoa Porridge

Lunch: Chickpea and Avocado Lettuce Wraps

Dinner: Baked Cod with Turmeric and Coconut Milk Sauce

Dessert: Raspberry Chia Seed Jam Tart

Day 5

Breakfast: Kale and Sweet Potato Breakfast Skillet

Lunch: Grilled Chicken and Quinoa Stuffed Bell Peppers

Dinner: Lemon and Herb Baked Chicken with Brussels Sprouts

Dessert: Coconut Macaroons with Dark Chocolate Drizzle

Day 6

Breakfast: Mushroom and Kale Omelette

Lunch: Shrimp and Cucumber Salad with Citrus Vinaigrette

Dinner: Spaghetti Squash with Walnut Pesto and Grilled Chicken

Dessert: Pumpkin Spice Chia Pudding

Day 7

Breakfast: Chia Seed Pudding with Fresh Berries

Lunch: Asian-Inspired Salmon Salad with Sesame-Ginger Dressing

Dinner: Cauliflower Steaks with Chimichurri Sauce

Dessert: Spiced Apple and Almond Crisp

Day 8

Breakfast: Coconut and Flaxseed Pancakes with Warm Berry Compote

Lunch: Lentil and Kale Salad with Lemon-Tahini Dressing

Dinner: Herb-Crusted Cod with Garlic Green Beans

Dessert: Matcha Green Tea Coconut Ice Cream

Day 9

Breakfast: Collard Green Breakfast Wraps with Turkey Sausage

Lunch: Roasted Beet and Arugula Salad with Walnuts and Goat Cheese

Dinner: Moroccan-Spiced Lamb with Cauliflower Couscous

Dessert: Coconut and Lime Energy Bites

Day 10

Breakfast: Avocado and Spinach Smoothie Bowl

Lunch: Grilled Veggie and Quinoa Stuffed Zucchini Boats

Dinner: Lemon-Garlic Shrimp with Zucchini Noodles

Dessert: Raw Cacao and Avocado Mousse

Day 11

Breakfast: Buckwheat Pancakes with Blueberry Compote

Lunch: Chickpea and Avocado Lettuce Wraps

Dinner: Roasted Chicken with Sweet Potatoes and Brussels Sprouts

Dessert: Baked Pears with Cinnamon and Walnuts

Day 12

Breakfast: Almond Butter and Banana Smoothie

Lunch: Shrimp and Cucumber Salad with Citrus Vinaigrette

Dinner: Cauliflower Steaks with Chimichurri Sauce

Dessert: Raspberry Chia Seed Jam Tart

Day 13

Breakfast: Coconut Flour Waffles with Berry Compote

Lunch: Grilled Chicken and Quinoa Stuffed Bell Peppers

Dinner: Lemon-Herb Grilled Tofu with Quinoa Pilaf

Dessert: Coconut Macaroons with Dark Chocolate Drizzle

Day 14

Breakfast: Chia Seed Pudding with Fresh Berries

Lunch: Lentil and Kale Salad with Lemon-Tahini Dressing

Dinner: Grass-Fed Beef Stir-Fry with Broccoli and Cauliflower Rice

Dessert: Pumpkin Spice Chia Pudding

Day 15

Breakfast: Quinoa Breakfast Bowl with Blueberries and Almond Butter

Lunch: Mediterranean Chickpea Salad with Cucumber and Feta

Dinner: Baked Cod with Turmeric and Coconut Milk Sauce

Dessert: Spiced Apple and Almond Crisp

Day 16

Breakfast: Smoked Salmon and Avocado Omelette

Lunch: Asian-Inspired Salmon Salad with Sesame-Ginger Dressing

Dinner: Spaghetti Squash with Walnut Pesto and Grilled Chicken

Dessert: Matcha Green Tea Coconut Ice Cream

Day 17

Breakfast: Almond Butter and Banana Smoothie

Lunch: Chickpea and Avocado Lettuce Wraps

Dinner: Lemon-Garlic Shrimp with Zucchini Noodles

Dessert: Coconut and Lime Energy Bites

Day 18

Breakfast: Pumpkin-Spiced Quinoa Porridge

Lunch: Grilled Chicken and Avocado Salad with Lemon-Basil Vinaigrette

Dinner: Roasted Chicken with Sweet Potatoes and Brussels Sprouts

Dessert: Raw Cacao and Avocado Mousse

Day 19

Breakfast: Kale and Sweet Potato Breakfast Skillet

Lunch: Grilled Veggie and Quinoa Stuffed Zucchini Boats

Dinner: Lemon and Herb Baked Chicken with Brussels Sprouts

Dessert: Baked Apple Slices with Cinnamon and Almonds

Day 20

Breakfast: Mushroom and Kale Omelette

Lunch: Lentil and Kale Salad with Lemon-Tahini Dressing

Dinner: Herb-Crusted Cod with Garlic Green Beans

Dessert: Raspberry Chia Seed Jam Tart

Day 21

Breakfast: Chia Seed Pudding with Fresh Berries

Lunch: Shrimp and Cucumber Salad with Citrus Vinaigrette

Dinner: Moroccan-Spiced Lamb with Cauliflower Couscous

Dessert: Coconut Macaroons with Dark Chocolate Drizzle

Day 22

Breakfast: Coconut and Flaxseed Pancakes with Warm Berry Compote

Lunch: Chickpea and Avocado Lettuce Wraps

Dinner: Cauliflower Steaks with Chimichurri Sauce

Dessert: Pumpkin Spice Chia Pudding

Day 23

Breakfast: Collard Green Breakfast Wraps with Turkey Sausage

Lunch: Grilled Chicken and Quinoa Stuffed Bell Peppers

Dinner: Lemon-Garlic Shrimp with Zucchini Noodles

Dessert: Spiced Apple and Almond Crisp

Day 24

Breakfast: Avocado and Spinach Smoothie Bowl

Lunch: Mediterranean Chickpea Salad with Cucumber and Feta

Dinner: Grass-Fed Beef Stir-Fry with Broccoli and Cauliflower Rice

Dessert: Matcha Green Tea Coconut Ice Cream

Day 25

Breakfast: Buckwheat Pancakes with Blueberry Compote

Lunch: Lentil and Kale Salad with Lemon-Tahini Dressing

Dinner: Spaghetti Squash with Walnut Pesto and Grilled Chicken

Dessert: Coconut and Lime Energy Bites

Day 26

Breakfast: Almond Butter and Banana Smoothie

Lunch: Grilled Chicken and Avocado Salad with Lemon-Basil Vinaigrette

Dinner: Baked Cod with Turmeric and Coconut Milk Sauce

Dessert: Raw Cacao and Avocado Mousse

Day 27

Breakfast: Coconut Flour Waffles with Berry Compote

Lunch: Asian-Inspired Salmon Salad with Sesame-Ginger Dressing

Dinner: Lemon-Herb Grilled Tofu with Quinoa Pilaf

Dessert: Raspberry Chia Seed Jam Tart

Day 28

Breakfast: Chia Seed Pudding with Fresh Berries

Lunch: Chickpea and Avocado Lettuce Wraps

Dinner: Lemon and Herb Baked Chicken with Brussels Sprouts

Dessert: Pumpkin Spice Chia Pudding

Day 29

Breakfast: Quinoa Breakfast Bowl with Blueberries and Almond Butter

Lunch: Shrimp and Cucumber Salad with Citrus Vinaigrette

Dinner: Cauliflower Steaks with Chimichurri Sauce

Dessert: Coconut Macaroons with Dark Chocolate Drizzle

Day 30

Breakfast: Smoked Salmon and Avocado Omelette

Lunch: Grilled Veggie and Quinoa Stuffed Zucchini Boats

Dinner: Moroccan-Spiced Lamb with Cauliflower Couscous

Dessert: Spiced Apple and Almond Crisp

This 30-day plan balances a variety of meals that align with the Good Energy principles, ensuring a mix of nutrients and flavors while supporting metabolic health and overall wellness.

Recipes Index

Almond and Cinnamon Spiced Coffee   95

Almond and Date Bars with Coconut Flakes   75

Almond and Date Energy Balls 59

Almond Butter and Banana Smoothie   20

Almond Flour Crackers with Olive Tapenade   66

Anti-Inflammatory Turmeric Latte   89

Asian-Inspired Salmon Salad with Sesame-Ginger Dressing   40

Avocado and Spinach Smoothie Bowl   24

Avocado and Tomato Salsa with Plantain Chips 71

Baked Apple Slices with Cinnamon and Almonds   83

Baked Cod with Turmeric and Coconut Milk Sauce   45

Baked Kale Chips with Sea Salt 67

Baked Pears with Cinnamon and Walnuts   76

Baked Sweet Potato Fries with Spicy Avocado Dip   64

Berry and Ginger Detox Smoothie   90

Blueberry and Basil Infused Water   94

Braised Lamb Shanks with Root Vegetables   49

Buckwheat Pancakes with Blueberry Compote   23

Cauliflower and Carrot Mash   62

Cauliflower Steaks with Chimichurri Sauce   58

Chia Seed Pudding with Fresh Berries   84

Chickpea and Avocado Lettuce Wraps   32

Coconut and Flaxseed Pancakes with Warm Berry Compote   15

Coconut and Lime Energy Bites 85

Coconut Chia Pudding with Mango   73

Coconut Flour Waffles with Berry Compote   27

Coconut Macaroons with Dark Chocolate Drizzle   74

Coconut Yogurt with Fresh Berries and Hemp Seeds   19

Collard Green Breakfast Wraps with Turkey Sausage   17

Cucumber and Carrot Sticks with Spicy Tahini Dip   60

Cucumber and Dill Greek Yogurt Dip   65

Cucumber and Mint Infused Water   88

Cucumber-Lemon Detox Water 96

Deviled Eggs with Avocado and Paprika68

Egg White Veggie Scramble with Fresh Herbs   28

Eggplant and Bell Pepper Caponata with Fresh Herbs   39

Golden Milk Turmeric Latte   91

Grass-Fed Beef Stir-Fry with Broccoli and Cauliflower Rice   47

Green Detox Juice with Spinach, Cucumber, and Ginger 92

Grilled Chicken and Avocado Salad with Lemon-Basil Vinaigrette   34

Grilled Chicken and Quinoa Stuffed Bell Peppers   30

Grilled Salmon with Quinoa and Avocado Salsa 41

Grilled Veggie and Quinoa Stuffed Zucchini Boats   37

Herb-Crusted Cod with Garlic Green Beans   52

Hibiscus and Rosehip Iced Tea 93

Kale and Sweet Potato Breakfast Skillet 26

Lemon and Herb Baked Chicken with Brussels Sprouts 50

Lemon-Coconut Energy Balls   79

Lemon-Garlic Shrimp with Zucchini Noodles   56

Lemon-Herb Grilled Tofu with Quinoa Pilaf   48

Lentil and Kale Salad with Lemon-Tahini Dressing   29

Matcha Green Tea Coconut Ice Cream   81

Matcha Green Tea with Almond Milk and Cinnamon   87

Mediterranean Chickpea Salad with Cucumber and Feta 35

Minted Green Iced Tea 97

Moroccan-Spiced Lamb with Cauliflower Couscous   53

Mushroom and Kale Omelette   22

Pumpkin Spice Chia Pudding   82

Pumpkin-Spiced Quinoa Porridge   25

Quinoa Breakfast Bowl with Blueberries and Almond Butter   13

Quinoa Porridge with Cinnamon and Walnuts   21

Raspberry Chia Seed Jam Tart   78

Raw Cacao and Avocado Mousse   77

Roasted Beet and Arugula Salad with Walnuts and Goat Cheese 31

Roasted Butternut Squash and Quinoa Pilaf with Cranberries   51

Roasted Chicken with Sweet Potatoes and Brussels Sprouts   55

Roasted Garlic and Avocado Hummus   61

Roasted Red Pepper Hummus with Veggie Sticks   63

Shrimp and Cucumber Salad with Citrus Vinaigrette   33

Smoked Salmon and Avocado Omelette 16

Spaghetti Squash with Walnut Pesto and Grilled Chicken   46

Spiced Apple and Almond Crisp   80

Spiced Golden Milk with Coconut Milk 98

Conclusion

As we come to the end of this journey together, I want to say how grateful I am that you've chosen to explore the world of Good Energy with me. Writing this cookbook has been a labor of love, born from my own experiences of learning how to nourish my body and mind in a way that supports my best self.

Living with Good Energy isn't about perfection or following a rigid set of rules. It's about making choices, day by day, that align with how you want to feel—vibrant, alive, and full of energy. It's about embracing food that not only tastes good but also does good for your body. It's about finding joy in the little things, whether that's a delicious meal, a peaceful moment, or the satisfaction of taking care of yourself and your loved ones.

I hope the recipes and tips in this book inspire you to create your own version of a Good Energy lifestyle, one that fits seamlessly into your life and brings you closer to feeling your best. Remember, it's not about drastic changes but rather about making small, sustainable shifts that add up over time.

Thank you for joining me on this journey. I hope you feel empowered to take what you've learned and make it your own. Here's to a life full of Good Energy, delicious food, and the joy of living well.

Bonus

Because we care so much about our readers and to ensure you get the best possible value of this Good Energy Cookbook, my team and I have provided kids-friendly good energy delicious recipes for your kids and for absolutely **FREE**

To gain access, all you have to do is use your mobile device to scan the QR code below or use the link below. Enjoy!

https://drive.google.com/drive/folders/18yaByzr1yd CraU7WduJU3UQLivAbPF0Y

Dear Reader, wait, just before you go,
Did you enjoy reading this book?

PLEASE CAN YOU CONSIDER LEAVING US YOUR FEEDBACK?

Your feedback is incredibly important to me and helps other readers discover my work. If you enjoyed the book and you have 60 seconds, it would mean a lot to me if you could leave a quick review on Amazon.

It's good for the book and I'd love to know how you benefited from it. I really appreciate you taking the time to read this book. This means a lot to me, I do not take it for granted.

Here's how you can do it:
Click on the book's title to go to its detailed page.
Scroll down until you find the "Customer Reviews" section.

You'll see a button that says "Write a customer review." Click on it.
You'll be asked to give the book a star rating from 1 to 5 stars. Give your honest rating
Share your thoughts about the book. What did you enjoy? What stood out to you? Your honest feedback is appreciated!

After writing your review, click the "Submit" button.
Your review will be posted on the book's Amazon page and will help other readers make an informed decision.
Thank you so much for your support!

THANK YOU!
Best regards,
Jenkins.

THE COMPLETE
GOOD
ENERGY
COOKBOOK
101 Metabolic-Boosting Recipes to
Optimize Your Health for Longevity
and Feel Incredible at Every Age

Dr. Rachel
Jenkins

Made in the USA
Las Vegas, NV
05 October 2024

96336705R00063